Hard to reach or out of reach?

AN EVALUATION OF AN INNOVATIVE MODEL OF HIV OUTREACH HEALTH EDUCATION

Hard to reach or out of reach?

AN EVALUATION OF AN INNOVATIVE MODEL OF HIV OUTREACH HEALTH EDUCATION

Tim Rhodes, Janet Holland
and Richard Hartnoll

the Tufnell Press

the Tufnell Press,
47 Dalmeny Road,
London, N7 0DY

First published December 1991

A catalogue record for this book is available
from the British Library

ISBN 1 872767 01 X

Jacket design by Dinusha Perera

Printed in England by Da Costa Print, London

Contents

FIGURES

ACKNOWLEDGEMENTS

This book is based upon an evaluation of an HIV outreach intervention in central London - Central London Action on Street Health (CLASH). We are grateful to the past and present outreach workers at CLASH without whose co-operation and assistance this research would not have been possible. In particular, we thank David Ayres, Ismail Bingor, Yvonne Butler, Jimi Christmas, Allison Culverwell, Marge Glynn, Nicolena Higgins and Michèle Lazarus. For information on CLASH other than that detailed here, the project can be contacted direct at CLASH, 15 Bateman Buildings, Soho Hospital, Soho Square, London, W1V. We also thank those involved in the setting up and management of the CLASH project for their time and comments during interview.

The evaluation was carried out as part of a larger study funded by the Department of Health to investigate the feasibility of outreach health education as a means of preventing HIV infection. We are grateful for the generous support provided by the Department of Health, and in particular to Liza Catan and Anne Kauder of the Research Management Division. We are also grateful to Anne Johnson (University College and Middlesex School of Medicine) for her comments, supervision and support throughout the study as a whole.

We thank those providing information on similar outreach interventions throughout the UK. In particular we thank the following for allowing permission to reproduce material relating to their respective outreach projects: Russell Newcombe and Tim Miller (Drugs and HIV Monitoring Unit, Mersey Regional Health Authority); Hilary Kinnell (Central Birmingham Health Authority); Terry Roberts (Plymouth Health Authority); and Jo Adams (Sheffield AIDS Education Project).

The research project was based at the Department of Politics and Sociology at Birkbeck College, University of London. We are particularly grateful to Susanne MacGregor for comments on an earlier draft, to Harriet Lodge for administrative assistance and to Terry Mayer for proof-reading. Finally we thank the Department of Health for financial assistance with production and publication and Robert Albury of the Tufnell Press.

The researchers can be contacted at the HIV Outreach Research Project, 16 Gower Street, London, WC1E 6DP.

July 1991

CHAPTER ONE

INTRODUCTION

The evaluation of CLASH was conducted as part of a three year Department of Health (DoH) funded study investigating outreach health education as a means of preventing HIV infection among hard-to-reach populations. The research project had three objectives: to review models of HIV outreach health education in Europe and the United States (US) (Rhodes *et al.*, 1990; 1991a); to conduct a survey of HIV outreach interventions in the United Kingdom (Hartnoll *et al.*, 1990; Rhodes *et al.*, 1991b); and to evaluate an innovative model of outreach health education in central London - Central London Action on Street Health (CLASH).[1] This book describes the evaluation. We have provided a summary report outlining the main findings from the research project as a whole elsewhere (Rhodes *et al.*, 1991c).

HIV prevention and outreach intervention

There are certain populations who are unlikely to be effectively reached by conventional HIV prevention strategies of health education, health promotion, counselling, sexually transmitted disease (STD) services, and drug advice agencies. These include hard-to-reach populations within the traditionally more difficult to access groups of injecting drug users, women and men working in the sex industries, homeless or transient young people, and their sexual partners. For example, it has been estimated that half of Britain's drug users are not in contact with treatment or helping agencies (Hartnoll and Power, 1989; Drug Indicators Project, 1989). It has also been found that those not in contact with helping agencies are more likely to be engaging in HIV transmission behaviours (Power *et al.*, 1988; Stimson *et al.*, 1988).

Although the hard-to-reach are a relatively small proportion of the total population, they are likely to be important in the transmission dynamics of HIV (Des Jarlais and Friedman, 1987; Padian, 1988). This arises both from the prevalence and frequency of HIV transmission behaviours which occur among them (Coleman and Curtis, 1989) and from their high level of mobility and interchange, occurring across different social networks and geographical areas (McDermott, 1988).

In response, there has been an increasing interest in the development and implementation of 'innovative' HIV prevention programmes, often based outside formal health service settings, with an emphasis on 'community-oriented' and 'user-friendly' approaches. Over the last two or three years HIV outreach intervention strategies have proliferated. Outreach has quickly come to be viewed as an essential, if not central, component of wider HIV prevention initiatives. But despite the sense of urgency which has surrounded the emergence of HIV outreach in the United Kingdom, a lack of descriptive and evaluative material remains, and little is known about the nature and comparative efficacy of differing interventions. We hope that this and previous reports will redress some of this imbalance by providing a national and international context for the interpretation of findings and by facilitating the design and implementation of future interventions.

Definitions of HIV outreach health education

For the purposes of our research, we have defined HIV related outreach health education as follows (Rhodes *et al.*, 1991c):

> "A community oriented activity with the overall aim of facilitating improvement in health and reduction in the risk of HIV transmission for individuals and groups from particular populations who are not effectively reached by existing services or through traditional health education channels".

The means of achieving these aims are based on identifying gaps in existing service provision and providing effective health education and services to populations within the community not yet adequately covered. HIV related outreach can thus be directed towards two target groups:

i.   individuals or groups considered vulnerable to HIV infection as a result of engaging in particular transmission behaviours, for example drug injectors and sex industry workers;

ii. populations or communities not defined primarily in terms of specific transmission behaviours but thought to be at increased risk due to the failure of communication of appropriate health education messages through existing channels, for example young people and specific ethnic minority groups.

Within this broad definition of outreach, there are two sub-divisions: detached and peripatetic outreach.

Detached work is undertaken outside any agency setting, for example work undertaken on the streets, station concourses, in pubs and cafes. This may aim either to effect risk reduction change 'directly' (*in situ*) in the community, or to facilitate change 'indirectly' by attracting individuals into existing treatment and helping services.

Peripatetic work focuses on organisations rather than on individuals, for example work undertaken in prisons, syringe exchanges, hostels and youth clubs. Peripatetic outreach places emphasis on broadening the range of people who are reached with health education messages, expanding their knowledge about available services, and training other workers and staff.

Outreach intervention and health promotion

The increased interest in community-oriented and community based approaches to health education and service provision over the last decade has led to challenges to conventional models of disease prevention associated with bio-medical understandings of health and illness (Doyle, 1979; Brown and Margo, 1979; Crawford, 1977, 1980; McKeown, 1979). Historically rooted within medical and epidemiological traditions, these models emphasise the belief that disease can be prevented by identifying and removing a causative agent of disease (Jewson, 1975; Allsop, 1984). This has often meant regarding the individual - and the body - as the focus for medicalised scrutiny in the search for specific aetiologies of disease in order to prevent their onset, if not to provide their management or 'cure' (Armstrong, 1983; Foucault, 1973).

In the light of these ideas, prevention has often been defined and organised in a tri-partite fashion, and strategies of health education have aimed to perform three complementary functions (Tones *et al.*, 1990). At the level of primary prevention, health education functions to persuade people to adopt behaviours thought to reduce the likelihood of disease, its related harm, and to encourage utilisation of existing services ('health behaviour', 'harm reduction' and 'help-seeking behaviour'). At the level of secondary prevention, health education functions to persuade individuals to practise self-care and to comply with medical recommendation and treatment. At the level of tertiary prevention, health education functions to persuade individuals to comply with medical treatment and to adjust to the limitations of lifestyle imposed by the presence of illness.

Approaches to the prevention of HIV infection have recently made explicit the problems associated with such rigid conceptions of prevention, health education and health and illness. Conventional medicine has been unable to find automatic 'cures' or 'magic bullets', and both the production of HIV disease and compliance with risk reduction practices have been shown to relate more to social, cultural and environmental factors than simply to bio-medical ones. In this way, the practice of HIV prevention has been located in wider discussions about public health, 'public good' and individual liberties (Porter, 1986; Porter and Porter, 1988), and about social inequalities on aspects of gender, sexuality and race (Watney, 1988a; 1988b; Treichler, 1987; Patton, 1988; Holland *et al.*, 1990). Approaches to health education which focus purely on the individual are therefore less appropriate than approaches which aim to encompass ideas of community, social or environmental change.

The commitment to developing community-based responses to intervention has developed both from within and outside the National Health Service (NHS). From within the NHS, these moves have seen increased emphasis on community development approaches to health, focusing on community participation and consumer health needs. The establishment of a Professional and Community Development Division within the Health Education Authority (HEA) in 1988 and the passing of the Community Care Act in 1990 are both moves in this direction (Webster, 1991; Smithies and Webster, 1991). As a result, there has been a narrowing of divisions between 'external' approaches to community development (for example, NHS initiated) and 'internal' approaches (initiated within communities themselves), and each have begun to occupy the same organisational space. Community health and self-help initiatives arising from within the community have increasingly gained funding from the statutory sector rather than from the charity and voluntary sector, and have begun to view the aims of their work - such as community participation and the redressing of health inequalities - in similar terms to wider agendas such as those of the World Health Organisation (National Community Health Resource, 1989).

This commitment to the development of community-based approaches to health promotion has been accompanied by a proliferation of attempts to categorise the diversity of health education practice (Draper *et al.*, 1980; French and Adams, 1986; Homans and Aggleton, 1988; Tones, Tilford and Robinson, 1990; Tones, 1981; Tuckett, 1979). In general, four models have been distinguished: the 'information-giving' or 'preventive' model; the 'self-empowerment' model; the 'community-action' model; and the 'radical-political' or 'socially transformatory' model. In an attempt to understand the role of HIV related outreach health education in the wider context of health education practice, we draw on some of our previous work, and briefly go on to describe each of these health education models in turn, before outlining the apparent theoretical value of outreach over more conventional health education approaches.

Information-giving models
Information-giving models of health education employ bio-medical understandings of health and illness and are rooted in the traditional 'preventive' approach. The model gives priority to the provision of information based on the belief that there are causal links between individuals receiving health information messages and modifying their health behaviour. This model is epitomised by the classic K-A-B (knowledge-attitudes-behaviour) approach to health education and presumes the translation of information to behavioural modification to be a relatively unproblematic and rational process.

   In relation to the prevention of HIV related harm and problematic drug use, the British Government's main preventive response - the use of the mass media and advertising - is clearly rooted in this approach. That the translation of information into behavioural modification is indeed a problematic process has been borne out by the diversity of responses (many negative) to the various campaigns (Research Bureau Limited, 1989; Watney, 1988c; Rhodes and Shaughnessy, 1990; Power, 1989).

Self-empowerment models
Models of self-empowerment, which are also individualistic in orientation, are based on ideas of 'informed choice', and unlike information-giving approaches, aim to "improve health by developing people's ability to control their health status within their environmental circumstances" (French and Adams, 1986). They emphasise the facilitation of personal growth, self-empowerment and self-assertiveness.

   This approach to health education and behaviour change is employed in many HIV counselling centres in the UK (Silverman, 1990), but can also be found in community-based interventions. The 'bleach and teach' campaign organised by the Mid City Consortium to Combat AIDS in San Francisco aims to provide drug injectors with the means (bleach) to enable rational choices to be made about injecting behaviour in situations which might otherwise have impeded the ability to make such choices

(Feldman and Biernacki, 1988). The establishment of the syringe exchange as a user-friendly, community based service over the past three years in the UK, has also endorsed the principles of self-empowerment by providing individuals with the means to inject safely.

Self-empowerment initiatives like syringe exchange, however, may be only partially effective, helping individuals to cope with rather than to change their circumstances (Pearson, 1973), and are generally unable to meet the needs for wider community or collective change. There are, for example, many instances when equipment sharing may be both socially desired and socially acceptable - when injecting equipment or exchanges are unavailable, when being initiated into injecting, when intoxicated, when sharing with particular partners, when in particular settings and so on (Haw, 1985; Friedman *et al.*, 1986; Feldman and Biernacki, 1988). These problems are further compounded by the limited success which syringe exchanges have had in reaching hard-to-reach drug injectors and those most vulnerable to infection, and the considerable difficulties experienced in maintaining contact with these clients over time (Stimson *et al.*, 1988). In a similar fashion, low threshold methadone programmes, and some treatment-oriented outreach interventions (for example, the New Jersey Coupon Program [Jackson *et al.*, 1987]) may also be limited in scope. Although they can be seen as empowering in the sense of enabling individuals to use drugs more safely and to achieve a more stable level of social functioning, they may also minimise client autonomy by encouraging a dependency on treatment methods themselves. It is clear that there is often a need to extend beyond the boundaries of self-empowerment and individually focused interventions in order to acknowledge the social and cultural constraints on health behaviour and to instrument change socially in the community.

Community-action models
In contrast to models of self-empowerment, community-action models of health education recognise the need to account for social and community 'norms' and 'values' when attempting to modify health behaviour. They therefore aim "to enhance health by bringing about community change through collective action" (Aggleton, 1989), emphasising "self-organisation and mutual assistance" (Beattie, 1991).

The Chicago AIDS Community Outreach Intervention Project is perhaps the best established model of community-action outreach intervention. The model is founded on an established tradition of developing innovative community-based programmes designed to intervene and contain local outbreaks of heroin use and addiction (Hughes and Crawford, 1972). Based on a multi-method approach which combines the principles of medical epidemiology with those of community ethnography (Wiebel, 1988; 1991), the model has key factors which facilitate change collectively in target communities. The use of 'indigenous' outreach workers, who function as 'AIDS Prevention Advocates', facilitates access and communication with target groups. The use of community ethnographic methods, and of ethnographers as outreach workers, helps to identify community norms and values attached to certain HIV relevant behaviours, and assists in the design and formulation of appropriate health education responses and recommendations. Finally, the encouragement of clients to become AIDS Prevention Advocates themselves enhances feelings of social responsibility among their peers and stimulates a collective response to HIV prevention.

There are many other examples of community-action HIV prevention and outreach programmes (Rhodes *et al.*, 1991a), and such initiatives are well established in gay communities (Veenker, 1990). Some of the latter have remained completely community-based and have refused government subsidies (for example, Aides in France, the Gay Men's Health Crisis and the Stop AIDS Project in the USA), others have accepted subsidies and formed more general non-government organisations (for example, AIDS Hilfe Verein in Germany, AIDS Hilfe Schweiz in Switzerland and the Terrence Higgins Trust in the UK). Without the same pre-existing social and organisational networks, the extent to which community organisation has occurred among drug using communities has been limited. Self-help groups like ADAPT in New York (where impetus for organisation initially came from outside the drug using community), the Junkiebonden in the Netherlands (Friedman *et al.*, 1988), and the Deutsche AIDS Hilfe (Narimani, 1991) are, however, fast gaining momentum.

Radical-political models
Moving beyond community-action models, radical-political or socially transformatory models aim to bring about "far reaching social change throughout society" (Aggleton, 1989). In recognising the social and regulatory constraints on achieving harm reduction behaviour, these models aim to achieve social, fiscal, legislative or environmental change by triggering collective political action.

Approaches such as this have been made in the Netherlands by Red Thread (Verbeek and Van der Zijden, 1988) and in the United States by COYOTE (Call Off Your Old Tired Ethics) among women working as prostitutes (Delacoste and Alexander, 1988). Each of these groups view sex workers as having little power or opportunity to create safer working conditions and to promote safer sex within them because of the contradictions which exist between restrictive and punitive official and legal policy on the one hand, and social reality (the demand for commercial sex) on the other (Biersteker, 1990). Both groups have been involved in developing outreach programmes which take account of these situations: for example, the operation of 'safe houses' in Amsterdam (AIDSCOM, 1989), and 'Cal-PEP' in association with AWARE (Association for Women's AIDS Research and Education) in San Francisco (Cohen *et al.*, 1988) . Similarly, the activist organisation ACT-UP has been involved in politically oriented interventionist strategies among gay men and drug users, and was instrumental in setting up the first syringe exchange in New York despite laws outlawing its existence (Sorge, 1991; Gillman, 1989).

Prescription to participation and the place of outreach

Using a framework which characterises prevention policies in terms of the extent to which they are imposed from above by institutions of authority or negotiated from within the affected communities concerned, Beattie and others have demonstrated how 'bottom-up' and 'top-down' health interventions often come to be polarised to varying extents at either ends of the authority-negotiation spectrum (Beattie, 1986; 1991; Hardy, 1981). Bottom-up interventions tend to start with the health priorities of communities and involve them as active participants in the process of education, prevention and change, and have been shown to have most in common with health education models of social and community change, such as community-action and radical-political models. Top-down interventions tend to reflect the issues and goals defined as important by health educators and policy makers, and have most in common with 'preventive' models of health education such as information-giving, and to a lesser degree, self-empowerment models. In this general sense, interventions which 'come from above' may be seen as impositions of policy and as inappropriate - sometimes even irrelevant - to the 'people below'. The above review of health education practice indicates that the possibilities for the focus (who) and mode (how) of intervention are poised between those which invite individualism, authoritarianism and prescription on the one hand and those which invite collectivism, negotiation and participation on the other.

These contradictory positions have often become embedded in approaches to health education themselves. The increased interest in community development has encouraged a convergence of approaches between those emerging from within communities themselves and those developed from outside communities by the statutory sector, local and central government and 'authority'. Whilst on one level this has meant an element of intersectoral collaboration, it has also brought into conflict many deep-seated, opposing and competing viewpoints from the variety of theoretical positions involved. The emergence and subsequent decline of the HEA's Professional and Community Development Division provides an example: not two years after it was established, the Division was disbanded, its potential contribution to achieving what could be termed 'community development' effectively controlled and minimised, and restrictions enforced on the publication of independent evaluation findings of its community development strategy (Smithies and Webster, 1991; Webster, 1991).

'Outreach' (as defined above), although often conforming to the principles of self-empowerment as opposed to community-action, can be seen historically to have more in common with bottom-up approaches to health than with top-down approaches (Rhodes and Hartnoll, 1991). Outreach thus contrasts sharply with conventional modes of health education which remain the dominant paradigms for HIV education and prevention (Homans and Aggleton, 1988; Friedman *et al.*, 1990). It has as one of its fundamental aims to identify, reach and provide services according to clients' expressed needs, where existing and more conventional health education approaches appear either inappropriate or irrelevant. In even its most conventional forms, outreach accepts the need for context specific health education, active participation on the part of the client, and recognises that accurate information alone may do little to modify behaviour (Gatherer *et al.*, 1987). In doing so, outreach aims to place health education in the context of individuals' social environments and in the context of social and health inequalities, aiming to explicitly involve clients and communities in the implementation of service responses to ensure that they are appropriate to a range of client and community needs.

Outreach has historically evolved from a range of community-based responses including philanthropy, self-help, social and political reform and community development for health. But like the historical development of community development itself (Webster, 1991), approaches to HIV related outreach are increasingly emerging from a combination of service perspectives, including combined top-down and bottom-up responses. In the United States for example, interventions operating from a combination of perspectives including community work, self-help, ethnography, epidemiological research and public health intervention are not unusual and may actually be the norm (Rhodes *et al.*, 1991b; Des Jarlais, 1989). In the United Kingdom, most HIV outreach projects remain situated in the voluntary sector (66 per cent in a recent survey, Hartnoll *et al.*, 1990), but projects are increasingly being established within statutory sectors, employing a mix of 'community' and 'professional' responses.

The increased intersectoral collaboration in relation to outreach work - or perhaps the increased involvement from established and 'professional' quarters about HIV-related outreach work - although reflecting wider trends of increased interest in community development as a whole, has its own unique sense of urgency and vociferousness. These moves may be significant in that the contradictory elements embodied in community development may be imported into the specific context of new outreach initiatives, but it may also suggest the potential for 'outreach' to become employed as an 'innovative' institutionalised response to community based HIV prevention.

Evaluation of Central London Action on Street Health (CLASH)

The evaluation of CLASH concentrated on the feasibility and effectiveness of project management functioning and of outreach service delivery. A summary of the evaluation findings, conclusions and recommendations can be found in Appendix A.

This book is divided into eight chapters, which need not be read sequentially. The aims and objectives of the evaluation, the evaluation methods used, and the main problems encountered in their use, are discussed in Chapter Two. The following chapter outlines the historical development of CLASH and the evolution and implementation of project aims and objectives. Findings concerned with the feasibility and effectiveness of the project's management structure and functioning are presented in Chapter Four and discussed and evaluated in Chapter Five, while findings relating to the project's detached outreach work, service delivery and client contact are presented in Chapter Six and discussed and evaluated in Chapter Seven. Chapters Four and Five, and Chapters Six and Seven in particular may be read as separate units in accordance with readers' specific areas of interest, although it should be stressed that issues of management and of service delivery are best viewed as inseparable. Some repetition between the main chapters is inevitable, given that the same information is relevant to history, practice and organisational structure, but an attempt has been made to minimise this by referring the reader to other relevant sections of the study. Finally, Chapter Eight draws the overall conclusions from the study and discusses their implications for the development of future outreach policy and practice.

CHAPTER TWO

METHODS OF EVALUATION

In this chapter we outline the methods of investigation employed in the study and describe the problems encountered in their application in relation to achieving evaluation objectives.

Evaluation of HIV outreach intervention

Evaluation aims to assess the feasibility, effectiveness and efficiency of an intervention in achieving stated aims and objectives. The evaluation process can be divided into four components: the evaluation and assessment of clients' needs; the monitoring of baseline information and the measurement of change; the evaluation of an intervention's implementation and process functioning; and the evaluation of an intervention's impact and outcomes. In general, evaluations are either process or outcome oriented. Broadly speaking, outcome evaluations are concerned with assessing the consequences of interventions, whether these are intended positive outcomes or unintended negative outcomes. Process evaluations tend to describe the context in which the intervention occurs and the processes involved in arriving at particular outcomes.

In assessing the outcomes of HIV outreach interventions the final arbiter is measurement of the intervention's impact on the rate of new HIV infections among targeted populations. However, such idealised studies of serial HIV measurement in cohorts are rarely, if ever, possible. Even if they were, problems in the interpretation of findings would remain, as any change in the rates of infection may be attributable to factors other than outreach.

In assessing outcomes of educational interventions the use of intermediate measures, such as assessments of changes in knowledge, attitudes and behaviour in target populations, are more commonly employed. This may be accomplished by using duplicate cross-sectional surveys before and after the intervention, with or without a comparison group not subjected to the intervention, and cohort studies of those receiving the intervention. However, the difficulties of assessing the impact of outreach *per se* on knowledge, attitudes or behaviour against a background of interventions from a range of sources can not be over-estimated. The frequently transient nature of outreach contacts and of hard-to-reach populations makes formalised methods of randomised evaluation and follow-up usually inappropriate. For this reason, those who participate in cohorts may not be representative of target populations, while comparison groups may have been dissimilar to the study group with respect to their behaviour prior to the intervention. Behaviour change measured by serial cross-sectional studies may be attributable either to the outreach intervention or to other concurrent health education campaigns.

As a result, outreach evaluation is often more focused on process than on outcome. At its most fundamental outreach evaluations may employ indirect measures of outcomes, such as descriptive monitoring to record the extent and nature of project activities. More sophisticated process performance indicators - which overlap to some degree with intermediate outcomes - include, for example, data on the extent of successful project referrals, take-up of services offered, rates of client re-contact, and knowledge of the project within targeted populations. Further to process performance monitoring, process evaluations usually use qualitative methods to describe and isolate the processes involved in the effectiveness and efficiency of project functioning. Such analyses are formative in nature and are capable of yielding ongoing recommendation for the improvement of working practices.

Evaluation of CLASH

The evaluation of CLASH began in early 1988 and ran until Autumn 1990. The aim of the evaluation was to assess the feasibility of CLASH as a model of outreach service delivery, and to explore the effectiveness of the project's outreach work as a means of preventing HIV infection. In doing this, the evaluation addressed three key questions of direct relevance for the design and implementation of future similar interventions:

i.   how feasible was the management and service structure adopted, and what lessons does the model have for informing future interventions?

ii. how valuable was the project in identifying and reaching hard-to-reach populations and in informing service responses according to client needs?

iii. what are the capabilities of outreach as a mode of health education
      and service delivery in terms of HIV prevention?

A combination of qualitative and quantitative methods were employed
to produce both an ethnographic and statistical account of CLASH and
its work. Given the nature of outreach work and of target populations, it
was not possible to obtain systematic direct measures of the impact of
the project on the rate of HIV infection or new HIV infections among
target populations, nor to evaluate directly the extent to which risk
reduction changes in target populations were attributable to the CLASH
intervention. Rather, a combination of approaches were employed. This
involved using process measures to describe and evaluate the project's
development, practice and performance, and using intermediate outcome
measures to describe and evaluate the extent and nature of client
outreach contact, outreach working practices and services provided.

The methods used in the evaluation are detailed below under the
sections headed 'intermediate outcomes evaluation' and 'process
evaluation'.

Intermediate outcomes evaluation

The aim of the intermediate outcomes evaluation was to assess the
outcomes or the consequences of the CLASH intervention, paying
particular attention to providing indicators of the effectiveness and
efficiency with which the CLASH project achieved its intended objectives.
The project's overall objective of reducing HIV transmission was broken
down into several intermediate goals which were assumed to contribute
to the achievement of this ultimate aim. The intermediate outcomes
evaluation thus focused on the extent to which specific outreach
strategies led to the achievement of specific intermediate objectives.
Intermediate outcome indicators included clients' HIV transmission
behaviour and behaviour change, referral take-up, use of services
offered and so on. These were supplemented further by indirect
indicators and process performance measures which were concerned
with the efficiency of service delivery. These included base-line measures
of the project's extent of contact with clients and with intended target
populations, and the extent of services offered.

Data sources and methods used

Statistical monitoring of the project's activities and of client characteristics
was undertaken using a variety of monitoring instruments.[1] These

included the systematic monitoring of the project's detached outreach work throughout the period 1st January 1988 to 31st July 1990 using new client contact sheets and re-contact client contact sheets. The collation of records held by a selection of CLASH's main referral points provided data on the extent to which client referrals made by CLASH were successful. Basic descriptive monitoring of the project's weekly activities as a whole was undertaken using random weekly timetables (RWTs). These were completed by each outreach worker one week in every four over two six monthly periods.

The main source of data for monitoring the detached outreach work was client contact sheets, although these were supplemented with data drawn from documentary material, interviews with past and present CLASH workers and with voluntary and statutory managers, and from participant observations in street detached settings (see below). The contact sheets, designed and piloted in close collaboration with the CLASH team, consisted of one contact sheet for each new client contacted, and one contact sheet for each re-contact with previously established clients. Both contact sheets were completed retrospectively by outreach workers shortly after completing outreach sessions. A separate and confidential list of client names, pseudonyms or 'descriptions' was held by the CLASH team to cross-reference with client identification numbers on contact sheets in order to provide ease of reference to particular clients, and to minimise the probability of duplicating client entries on new contact sheets. The contact sheets were designed to be as 'user-friendly' as possible to facilitate data entry, and were structured so as to allow the data to be transferred directly from contact sheets onto computer to eliminate any need for recoding and to minimise potential sources of data error.

The new client contact sheet aimed to elicit information on the number of clients contacted, the locations where contacts took place, the style and duration of contacts, whether clients were in contact with any other form of helping agency, indicators of clients' HIV transmission behaviour, services offered and issues discussed, and the extent and nature of client referrals. Client re-contact sheets duplicated only a selection of core questions from the new contact sheet and included further items on clients' behaviour change and outcome of any previous referrals.

The data from both the new client contact sheet and the re-contact sheet were analysed using SPSSx.[2] Statistical test results have been omitted from the text below. When statistically 'significant' associations or differences are cited these refer to probabilities of at least $p < 0.05$.

Note on intermediate outcomes evaluation

In practice, there were problems encountered in applying the intermediate outcome measures, even with the most indirect of indicators such as the process performance measures. Although the contact sheets for example, were thorough - if not exhaustive - in the questions they posed, the realities of detached outreach work introduced a number of problems for the systematic monitoring of client contacts and project activities.

The status of data gathering in outreach work, although vital to informing appropriate service responses, was considered by outreach workers secondary to making contacts and providing necessary services. Outreach contacts were often brief and hasty. Target clients were sometimes initially suspicious of outreach workers, justifiably saw lengthy interventions as interference, and occasionally simply rebuffed approaches from workers altogether. The outreach contact between client and worker therefore often needed to remain as understated as possible, so as not to draw the attention of police, punters, pimps or 'boyfriends' (see also Chapter Six).

In these circumstances, the act of establishing the new contact and of entering into initial conversation was the outreach worker's first priority, and data gathering came second. Unlike most research interventions, client information may not have been 'actively' sought unless it was thought by outreach workers to be vital to the contact itself, while on the other hand information thought potentially disruptive to clients - no matter what its value for evaluation purposes or indeed for long term work with clients (such as HIV antibody status) - may have been actively avoided (fieldnotes, 1990). From a research perspective, the selectivity of the information gathered poses problems for the reliability of the data, as there is an increased likelihood of uncertainty about the information considered most sensitive to clients by the outreach workers conducting the outreach contacts.

Similarly, whether or not the outreach workers informed their clients that monitoring information was being gathered depended on whether workers perceived this knowledge to be disruptive to establishing contacts. For these reasons, data - especially on initial contacts with clients - was often gathered by outreach workers in a covert rather than overt manner to minimise the 'threats' potentially posed to the outreach contact by the client's knowledge of being researched. It was more likely that clients became aware of the monitoring of information on subsequent contacts and as their contact with the project became more established. Once again, from a research perspective this situation may introduce problems. It may be considered unethical to gain statistical information about clients covertly, especially given the illegal nature of some client activities. In this respect, while the CLASH project were taking part in the monitoring of their outreach work for the dual purposes of independent evaluation and project recording, it was entirely the team's decision whether clients would be informed of this.

The reliability of data is further compounded by the extent and efficiency with which outreach workers recorded client information. Contact sheets were completed retrospectively by outreach workers, and would often not be completed immediately after outreach sessions as planned. This introduced the possibility of confusion about client details and sometimes about the actual numbers of clients contacted, especially if fieldnotes had not been made by workers after sessions. There is thus a possibility that an unknown number of contacts, especially fleeting contacts, went unrecorded. The brevity and style of some outreach contacts also meant that the amount of information ascertained was limited. As mentioned above, there was a high degree to which information on many of the intermediate outcome measures was unknown to outreach workers. On fleeting contacts often only basic demographic client characteristics could be recorded.

As might be expected, the degree to which individual workers participated in the evaluation process, and assisted in monitoring in particular, varied within the team, relating to individual beliefs and opinions about the evaluation, its purpose and potential implications (see also below).

For these reasons, the data gathered from contact sheets are not as reliable as the contact sheets might have allowed or that might have been collected had the sample been less 'opportunistic' or drawn from an agency or clinic based sample, and the numbers of clients recorded is probably a slight under-estimate. Nonetheless, the data recorded provides insight into the applicability and potential of such measures for the evaluation of outreach, gives adequate details on intermediate and indirect indicators, and allowed the CLASH team immediate access to records of their activities and details of their client group.

Process evaluation

The process evaluation aimed to describe the context in which the CLASH intervention occurred and to isolate the processes involved in the project arriving at particular outcomes. In short, whereas the intermediate outcomes evaluation aimed to investigate *what* the project achieved, the process evaluation aimed to explain *how* this was achieved.

The process evaluation involved documenting the historical development of the CLASH project, describing the project's objectives and the ways in which they evolved, and describing how the CLASH team functioned in terms of management and working practices.

Data sources and methods used

The data for the process evaluation was drawn from a variety of methods which were mostly qualitative in nature (See Patton, 1987, 1990). Background information on the origins and development of CLASH and of project objectives prior to the commencement of the evaluation were provided through the collation and analysis of documentary evidence of correspondence, minutes of meetings, proposals, progress and policy reports, fieldnotes of informal discussion, and through interviews (see below). These data were collected and analysed throughout the entire evaluation period.

Data relating to the management functioning of the CLASH project were provided primarily through interviews with selected key individuals from both statutory and voluntary health sectors, with current and former CLASH workers and with collaborating outreach workers, and through fieldnotes of informal discussion and observation. Eighteen interviews were undertaken throughout the first six months of 1990: seven with statutory sector representatives of Bloomsbury Health Authority (BHA)[3], four with voluntary sector representatives, and seven with past and present CLASH outreach workers. The interviews, which were tape-recorded and transcribed, were loosely structured, which allowed the interviewer to cover a basic agenda of issues and allowed interviewees to pursue areas of individual interest and importance. The interviews provided opportunities for in-depth discussion, and generally lasted between one and a half to two hours. Extracts reported from the interviews with statutory representatives are coded with '(s)', with voluntary representatives with '(v)', and with outreach workers with '(w)'.

The observations were undertaken at weekly project management and review meetings, at CLASH Steering Group management meetings, and at the CLASH office on average one day a week for one year. These focused on the efficiency and effectiveness of intra-team dynamics, in particular the process by which the team organised their work and how decisions were made, and of management functioning, in particular the problems encountered in the style of project management adopted.

Data relating to the project's outreach working practices were provided through documentary evidence of progress reports and policy papers, interviews with past and present CLASH workers and voluntary and statutory managers, fieldnotes of informal discussion, observations at the CLASH office, and through participant observations in street detached settings. These methods focused on the process by which outreach contacts were made, on the problems and difficulties encountered in undertaking detached work and in providing outreach services and client referral. Participant observations were undertaken on average once a week since May 1990. These focused on outreach sessions undertaken with rent boys in Victoria, but also included outreach sessions with rent boys in Piccadilly and Euston, and client drop-in sessions at the CLASH office. These methods were supplemented with fieldnotes from site visits to other selected UK outreach projects, and with indicators of project performance obtained through random weekly timetables, team log books and team diaries. The site visits were undertaken in Birmingham, Liverpool and Plymouth, and included discussion with outreach workers and outreach project managers and observations in street detached settings.

The functioning of the project's training and peripatetic outreach work was not formally evaluated, although basic descriptive data was collected.

Note on process evaluation

Process evaluation can not give the definitive 'true' story of the CLASH project. What it can do is provide the bones of the history and development of the project in terms of crucial events recorded in documentary and other sources fleshed out by both the actions and perceptions of critical actors and of other sources of information about the same events. As will become clear from the presentation of the data from the process evaluation, the critical actors involved perceived and understood events from a range of differing perspectives which had direct implications on the course of their actions in practice.

In the process evaluation two basic methods inform the interpretation of actors' accounts, particularly in the analysis of interview material. The first is to seek congruence - how does the account compare with other accounts of the same experience? The second is to explore coherence - how is the account itself organised in terms of internal coherence (Denzin, 1970)?

In the evaluation of CLASH we used multiple data collection strategies to build checks and balances into the research design, and provide internal validation for the ethnographic data. The overall strategy is referred to as triangulation. Denzin (1978) identifies four types of triangulation: (1) data triangulation, using a variety of data sources in a study; an example is interviewing people in different positions, or who have different perspectives; (2) investigator triangulation, using several different researchers; (3) theory triangulation, using multiple perspectives to interpret a set of data; and (4) methodological triangulation, using multiple methods to study a single problem, for example interviews, observation, questionnaires and documents (see Fielding and Fielding (1986) for a discussion and critique of a simplistic use of triangulation). The current study involved data, investigator and methodological triangulation. A variety of sources of data about CLASH were used; there were two investigators, who compared and discussed their interpretation and understanding of the events and issues under study; and a range of methods were used to collect information from the various sources.

The analysis of the qualitative data gathered in this way was an iterative process of immersion in the various data sources in order to develop categories of description and analysis, then returning to the data to check the meaningfulness of the categories produced in this process. The process involves what Guba (1978, 1981) has called the problems of convergence and divergence. The problem of convergence entails working out what things go together, and so generating the classification system, the set of categories with which to describe and analyse the data. Here one seeks recurring regularities in the data, and the resulting categories are judged on the 'internal homogeneity' - do the things in the category hold together in a meaningful way; and 'external heterogeneity' - are there clear differences between categories. The problem of divergence entails fleshing out the categories by extension (building on items of information already known), bridging (making connections between items) and surfacing (suggesting new information which would fit the analysis and checking its existence). The process in general is one of uncovering patterns, themes and categories in interaction with the data, and deciding what is significant. The capacity to do this is the basic skill required of the qualitative researcher.

The description of CLASH presented here emerges from a range of sources using a number of methods. The analysis and presentation of actors' differing perceptions provides the context for an understanding of the historical development of CLASH and alternative interpretations of that history, as it does the work of CLASH in the light of objectives and of the role of outreach work. It is of particular interest to note congruence and convergence in the accounts of critical actors discussed below -

convergence in the accounts of actors taking widely different initial positions for example - but also ways in which differing ideological positions produce very different interpretations of events.

Issues relating to the participant observation undertaken with CLASH in street detached settings, and the problems encountered in its negotiation, are discussed below. Participant observation was undertaken in detached outreach sessions with rent boys in Victoria and Piccadilly by one of the evaluators from May 1990. This work continues (1991). It was not possible for the research team to have access to clients in order to ascertain their views of the services offered to them (see below).

Relationship between CLASH and the research team

Here we outline the relationship between the CLASH workers and the research team in terms of the negotiation and practice of participant observation with rent boys in detached outreach work, and the feedback of research findings to CLASH workers, project managers and funders.

Participant observation in street detached settings
In order to provide an in-depth descriptive account of the applicability and relevance of CLASH's outreach service provision to target populations, and to complement base-line monitoring data, it was originally envisaged that one of the researchers might have access to clients. This would have allowed an opportunity to ascertain clients' perceptions of their need for outreach services and their views relating to the efficacy of the CLASH intervention. Although vital to an evaluation of this nature, in practice this proved unworkable.

There were changes in the research team personnel. The development of trust between the original researchers and the CLASH team, vitally important in a process evaluation of this type, had taken considerable time. With change in research personnel, continuity was broken and the process of relationship-building between the evaluator and the CLASH team had to be re-assessed and re-negotiated. At the time when the replacement researcher first began observation work at CLASH (early 1989) the team had already decided that there would be no research access to clients, and this was considered a high priority on the CLASH team's evaluation agenda. The atmosphere from a research point of view was immediately hostile, and the team were fast to map out the boundaries of the research as they saw them, and as they had previously been negotiated. It seemed that the CLASH team's position of 'no-access' was static and inflexible.

Occasional discussions - sometimes heated - took place, where the new researcher was able to put forward his perception of the problems and of the needs for research access to clients. Over time it became clear to the researcher that certain team members began to see the need for such research to assess clients' needs and views about service delivery and to inform appropriate service responses, but were still unable to reconcile this with their perceptions of outreach work and of client confidentiality, or with other workers' opinions which had remained unchanged.

The problem for workers, including those sympathetic to the needs of the research, seemed two-fold: sensitivity of worker-client relations; and preservation of client confidentiality. Given the transient nature of the client groups, and the length of time invested by the team to establish relationships with clients, there was a great deal of reluctance to expose what appeared already precarious relationships to one who was often considered an 'outsider'. This position, however, seemed equally rooted in a fear of exposure to a critical and uncontrollable gaze as it did to protecting sensitive client relationships from being disrupted. In the light of this, the view most often articulated by workers was that a 'researcher', regardless of experience and expertise in research or 'street scenes', was unable to be viewed in similar terms as 'workers': there was a qualitative and conceptual difference. Workers felt that should a researcher have access to clients, clients should be informed that it was a researcher, and that not to do so would be unethical and exploitative. Similarly, from a research perspective, it was considered far more satisfactory to conduct ethnographic work (observations, participant observations and interviews) overtly rather than covertly.

But for CLASH, to inform clients of the research (whether in participant observations or through conducting interviews) meant jeopardising relations between the project and their existing and future clients. Their reasons were three-fold. First, outreach contacts with new client contacts were very brief and often hastily undertaken, which meant there was a practical difficulty in raising the issue of participant observations or in introducing the researcher: the priority was to establish the contact with view to providing health education services. Second, outreach workers were often viewed initially with suspicion from new clients, and to inform clients that they were being researched would disrupt the opportunities available (however brief) for gaining trust from clients about the confidential nature of the work, which was considered a pre-requisite to effectively delivering services (especially when encouraging client referrals). Third, the team considered it inappropriate that the researcher should have access to established clients, even if these contacts were found not to be disrupted by the research, as knowledge about the fact that the CLASH service involved a research element might subvert the team's credibility when conducting new contacts on the street. The team therefore viewed direct research involvement with clients as a negative process, despite realising the formative value of research in assessing clients' needs and in developing services according to these requirements. This was felt to be the case whether the researcher was known merely to be collecting core statistical information about clients, doing street based observations or engaging in conversation or interviews with clients. Here, workers' views about the role of the researcher as being conceptually different to those of themselves is important: for example, workers were themselves collecting the statistical information about clients in a covert fashion, presumably without the ethical problems and the difficulties about client trust and confidentiality.

The problem of client confidentiality was therefore considered in relation to the sensitivity of worker-client relations, and as an ethical issue in itself. Whether or not granting research access to clients would be disruptive to the project's outreach work, the CLASH team had to be assured of absolute trust on behalf of the researcher regarding any information gleaned from client observations. This was also considered a fundamental tenet of the study from a research perspective. This, however, was an assurance the team felt they could not gain from the research, and an assurance they felt their clients could not assume. Once again, this view was embedded in the team's wider perceptions of the role of research as being conceptually different from their own, where it was viewed that only CLASH workers should have access to such information and only CLASH workers who could be trusted to keep such information confidential or to use such information in a responsible or meaningful manner. Where access to clients was concerned, without the 'researcher' actually being a 'worker', the CLASH team (at least initially) viewed the contribution of research as intrinsically problematic and questionable. While, from a research point of view, the issue of access to clients was considered delicate and problematic for many of these reasons (ethics, confidentiality, negotiation and ownership of information), it seemed the team's official line (which was contradicted by individual team members) often defied the logic of formative and negotiated evaluation, and indeed of community based prevention work, where assessing and responding to clients' expressed needs can be considered an axiomatic principle.

A number of factors appeared to influence and facilitate the process of negotiation. First, the researcher, through having spent almost one day a week at the CLASH office for a number of months, increasingly gained the trust of the CLASH team. This process had occurred through informal discussion in team settings as well as with individual workers. Second, the CLASH team became increasingly aware of the need for such research in the context of the evaluation. This latter point partly resulted from the increased need to meet requests from the project's Steering Group and funders for information relating to detached outreach work, and from the realisation of the value of base-line monitoring data provided by the researcher on such occasions. It became clearer to workers that the evaluation was both committed to generating useful information to inform the direction and development of outreach services, and that this was best achieved through the negotiation and participation with clients. Furthermore, for the evaluation to be considered authoritative by project managers, at least some members of the team felt the researcher required more than a distanced insight into the nature of detached outreach work. In this respect, some workers' opinions had turned full circle: from the position where access to clients and information was potentially dangerous to a position where knowledge and information was power. A third factor was that the team felt the need for more sessional workers, and had argued that the researcher, even without direct experience of detached work, at least had a working knowledge of the issues involved and of the project's working practices.

At a time when the researcher had long considered the possibility of gaining access to clients both unlikely and unworkable, and as data gathering on the evaluation project was nearing completion, the team offered the researcher sessional work with rent boys in Euston and Victoria. Once the offer had been made, three to four further months passed, during which time certain workers questioned the practicality of the idea (as did the researcher), before the terms of the proposal were either formulated or agreed.

The agreement was a highly conditional one, under which the researcher would regard himself, and be regarded by the project and clients as a sessional CLASH worker, not a researcher. This involved having an induction period into detached work with CLASH and being paid a sessional workers' fee (a factor objected to by some on the Steering Group), and was probably only realistic under these terms given that most data collection was completed (May 1990). Thus, the ethical problem of 'being a researcher' as far as the CLASH team were concerned was if not solved, at least avoided, almost by denial: now a worker, not a researcher. In practice, this meant that the researcher - when observing - was acting covertly and without a sufficiently negotiated research agenda. This arrangement, from a research point of view, might easily be seen as unrealistic and as potentially quite confusing: if observation was to inform the interpretation of evaluation findings, not only was it to be achieved covertly in relation to clients, but it was initially 'denied' any knowledge in practice. But the very act of 'becoming a worker' meant experiencing first-hand all that which other workers (especially sessional workers) had experienced, both in terms of doing outreach work and in terms of intra-team management and relations. Furthermore, once participant observation in detached work had begun, the boundaries between research and work and the unique value of this combination became clearer to both workers and the researcher, and in practice it was usual for most re-contacted clients to be informed of the fact that one of the outreach workers was also the project evaluator and that participant observations were taking place.

The detached sessions undertaken by the researcher and the first-hand experiences of being a worker, therefore, were able to lend a deeper qualitative understanding to the interpretation of evaluation findings, although were obviously unable to provide opportunities for overt discussion with clients about their perceptions, views and experiences of receiving outreach services as was originally intended. The researcher began weekly sessions with one full-time CLASH worker in May 1990, undertaking street detached sessions with rent boys initially in Euston. At the time of writing (mid 1991), and since the evaluation has been completed, he continues to work with CLASH as a sessional worker with rent boys in Victoria and Piccadilly.

Feedback of research findings to CLASH
The research team had provided no formal arrangement for regular feedback of research findings to the CLASH team or to their managers and funders. In practice, the researcher had considerable contact with CLASH when undertaking observational work in team meetings and at the CLASH office. This meant that feedback of selected findings were supplied usually upon demand. On a number of occasions statistical break-downs of core monitoring findings were provided, for example, for inclusion in the project's Bi-Annual Report (1989), for dissemination at BHA's 'HIV and AIDS Information Group' (1989-1990), for inclusion in the Health Authority's Regional Annual HIV Reports (1989), and in

response to a request for an interim progress report from the Monument Trust (1990) who were partially funding the project.

This evaluation report was also circulated in draft forms to CLASH team members and key people involved in the running and management of the project. At the time of writing, the findings and recommendations of the study are being used by CLASH to contribute towards developing future project strategy about practice and policy in a three month bi-annual project assessment and review (1991), and the evaluator has been invited by the CLASH team to undertake an advisory role to review and develop current systems of internal monitoring and feedback of project activities.

CHAPTER THREE

HISTORY AND DEVELOPMENT

Drawing on documentary evidence and interview material, in this chapter we give a description of the development of the aims and objectives of CLASH and a chronology of significant events in the project's history. Clearly there will be different perspectives on processes and events in individuals' accounts, and these will become evident later, but here we aim to describe the historical background of CLASH in order to provide a basis for the discussion and evaluation of findings contained in subsequent chapters.

Aims and objectives of CLASH

The original proposal for the CLASH project identified the target populations on which their efforts were to be focused and outlined three areas of work for the health outreach workers. At this time, the broad target group identified was young homeless people in central London. Within this, sub-groups thought to be at increased risk of contracting sexually transmitted diseases (STDs), particularly HIV infection, were to be targeted. These included women and men working in the sex industries, injecting drug users and gay and bisexual men.

The three areas of work identified for the project were:

i.   Outreach work. This would involve the workers making direct contact with individuals within intended target populations with the aim of offering help, information, advice and counselling on all aspects of health but particularly concerning HIV infection and HIV transmission;

ii. Development of health education materials. This would involve the project developing health education materials for target populations which were "accessible, relevant, appropriate and complementary to existing resources". It would also involve assessing the suitability and quality of existing materials;

iii. Facilitating access to health services. This would involve the project providing referrals for clients to existing appropriate medical and social services. Many of CLASH's target groups would normally not have access to such services, and might remain suspicious of them. This would require the project to liaise with potential health and social services in the area. It was envisaged that where necessary workers would accompany clients to services.

These broad project objectives have been maintained, but as will become clear in this and following chapters, the specific focus of the project's activities have changed over time, affected by a variety of factors including the changing interests and capacities of team members, the concerns of the Steering and Management Groups, practical experience and the focus and work of other similar agencies. The main shifts in focus and emphasis of the project's aims and objectives can be summarised as follows:

i.   Target populations. Throughout the developmental stages of project work, the original target group of young homeless people was seen as too large and in need of more precise focus. As a result, the team placed greater emphasis in their detached outreach work on targeting those at increased vulnerability to HIV transmission, largely men and women working in the sex industry and injecting drug users. Contact with the young homeless was continued through peripatetic outreach work with both staff and clients of agencies working with the young homeless, such as hostels, night shelters and day centres;

ii.   Methods of outreach contact. Initially much of CLASH's contact with clients was made in collaboration with other agencies, or through peripatetic outreach work. Increasingly, however, the project was able to establish its own direct contact with individual clients through detached outreach work and through the development of a client drop-in service, where health education, advice, condoms and injecting equipment were provided. In particular, detached outreach work with women working as prostitutes was established;

iii. Training. Having completed "a rolling programme of training with hostel workers" (CLASH, 1987), CLASH began to limit the direct provision of training to other services, preferring to increase networking and liaison with other services in order to facilitate access and referral for clients to relevant local services;

iv.   Direct and *in situ* service provision. There was a general move towards placing greater emphasis on direct and *in situ* service provision by CLASH. This involved providing clients with prevention materials such as condoms and injecting equipment, developing a client drop-in service, and putting forward proposals for greater community based service provision, such as a mobile outreach unit and a low threshold women's health centre based in King's Cross.[1]

Two years after CLASH was established, the project clarified their objectives as follows (Bi-Annual Report, 1989):

i. to contact those not in contact with health services or helping networks: the young homeless, drug users, drug injectors, women prostitutes, rent boys, and prisoners;

ii. to train workers in existing voluntary sector projects, for example hostels for the homeless;

iii. to provide and facilitate referrals to health services, voluntary organisations and social services, and to identify requirements for improved access to services and to service provision;

iv. to provide health education, advice and counselling, particularly concerning HIV infection and AIDS;

v. to provide prevention materials: syringes, needles, condoms, spermicides, and lubricants;

vi. to develop appropriate health education literature and materials.

These continue to be the principle objectives of the CLASH project. In the following chapters, the work of CLASH and the feasibility of the project as a model of outreach health education are considered in the light of the objectives outlined above. The historical background and development of CLASH plotted below provides the context in which the aims and objectives were formulated and implemented.

Historical background

In describing the historical background to the setting up and development of the CLASH project, we have distinguished four distinct periods: origins (1985-1986), early development (1987-1988), development (1988-1989), and moving on (1989-1990).

Origins: Birth of an idea [1985-1986]

CLASH was set up at a time when the NHS in general and BHA in particular were under considerable pressure and the institutional ethos was one of change. Part of this pressure, particularly in Bloomsbury, was the need to develop services to deal with the potential spread of HIV infection and AIDS. The issue of HIV and AIDS from a Health Service perspective represented both a threat and a challenge: what are the service needs, can they be met, and if so, how? It also represented opportunity - in a period of retrenchment due to contraction and financial constraint, the AIDS sector was one of the few growth sectors with relatively large national and regional resources still being made available.

Bloomsbury Health Authority was at the time a large, recently created (1982) complex organisation with a diverse social geography and "an elitist self image, with an emphasis on 'quality'", a place where reputations could be made (Ferlie and Pettigrew, 1988). As Ferlie and Pettigrew note, it seems to have had a reputation for being "a teaching district and slightly glamorous", attracting people who were interested in engaging in innovation, doing "interesting... remarkable projects" and then moving on. The other side of the coin was that there were not so many people who were keen to "do the boring bits, the more ordinary things that are not in the spotlight", and the Authority could also be described as "the shoddiest, least competent, shabbiest district... in terms of facilities and the ability to get its acts together" (s).[2] Put another way, "Bloomsbury used to be the place to get into, now it is the place to get out of" (Ferlie and Pettigrew, 1988).

The development of HIV and AIDS related services in Bloomsbury was influenced by two main factors: a demand for services and a pre-disposed willingness to supply them. From a very early stage in the HIV epidemic, there was a demand for services in Bloomsbury from people living with HIV infection and AIDS. The reported cases of AIDS in Bloomsbury give just one indicator of the extent of such demand: from three reported cases of AIDS in Bloomsbury in 1983, this figure had risen to over four hundred by March 1991.[3] Most commonly, the demand for services was concentrated around the Authority's STD clinics in the genito-urinary medicine (GUM) departments of University College Hospital (UCH) and the Middlesex Hospital at James Pringle House (JPH).

The willingness to supply HIV related services to meet this demand was already present. Clinicians and researchers, particularly in the GUM department at University College and Middlesex School of Medicine (UCMSM), were keen to develop a high profile in HIV related research and service development. These are both major teaching hospitals with strong academic departments enjoying national and international reputations, particularly in relation to HIV research. The Department of Virology at the Middlesex, for example, had been responsible for developing one of the world's first HIV antibody tests in 1985, while the Academic Department of GUM was involved in a range of HIV related social and medical research projects.

Against a background of rapid organisational change and political and strategic activity at national, district and local level, HIV and AIDS related service development in Bloomsbury had two elements: hospital based and community based services. The latter was increasingly perceived as having an important educative and preventive function. The District General Manager wrote to Region in August 1986:

"The pace of change in this service is very rapid given the growing numbers, and our requirements are being kept regularly under review. The District is conscious of the need to invest resources in education and prevention as well as in the in-patient and out-patient services, and we are currently examining the possibility of funding this year a community outreach programme..." (Ferlie and Pettigrew, 1988).

Much of the impetus for this particular development had been 'bottom up', developing out of the concerns and interests of those in the voluntary sector working with the young homeless. It was recognised that although the large, often transient population of young people in central London who were without secure accommodation and involved in drug taking or prostitution were more likely to come into contact with voluntary rather than statutory agencies, voluntary agencies were often without the necessary resources required to cater for their general health care and HIV-specific needs. In late 1985 representatives from several London voluntary agencies met with those from the Terrence Higgins Trust (THT) and Bloomsbury Health Authority's Academic Department of GUM, and the West End Coordinated Voluntary Services for Single People (WECVS).[4] Their objective was to consider a proposal to develop a model of outreach health education to reach young people in London who were without access to established primary care services and who were at increased risk of STDs, particularly HIV infection. The aim was to provide hard-to-reach clients with a service which delivered appropriate health education and prevention, as well as referral access into existing statutory and voluntary health and welfare services. The intention was thus to 'bridge' gaps in service provision between the two sectors. The voluntary agencies involved included the Soho Project[5], the Basement Project[6], the Hungerford Drug Project[7], the Blenheim Project[8] and the Piccadilly Advice Centre[9]. Each felt that they had the necessary experience and expertise to contribute to the development and management of such a project.

This initial meeting led to a further meeting in May 1986 of parties interested in pursuing and realising the proposal. The objective of this meeting was to decide on an appropriate structure for the project, to form a steering group and to consider possibilities for funding. At this point, two competing approaches to the organisation and structure of the project emerged. First, that the project should be developed from within existing voluntary agencies undertaking outreach work, and funding should be sought to expand these agencies in order to cater for this new, specific service. Second, that there should be one new project employing dedicated outreach health workers which would work independently while collaborating closely with existing outreach projects. There was also the question of whether this independent outreach project should be based within the voluntary or statutory sector.

The first approach, it was argued, would prevent the marginalisation of health work by integrating it into the ongoing work of existing agencies, and would provide a foundation of "existing contacts and existing client groups" from which to snowball when contacting target groups (v). A major disadvantage of this approach was that the work could be "swallowed up" amongst service and management practices of the existing agencies' (v). The alternative view regarded the independence of the new unit as crucial both to avoid this loss of autonomy and to ensure the precise targeting of the project's specific client groups. Despite considerable discussion, a decision could not be reached. The WECVS Steering Group delegated representatives of two of the voluntary agencies (Soho Project and Hungerford Drug Project) to make a decision, and committed themselves to accepting this decision. The group agreed to establish the project independent of existing agencies: "it was set up as a separate project which would primarily be an outreach project with the clinical support of Bloomsbury through its STD clinics, GPs and doctors.." (v). It was to be based in the statutory sector but was to have strong links and involvement with the voluntary sector. A Steering Group was established, at this point known as the WECVS Steering Group, which consisted of those attending the initial meetings, and work began on developing a proposal for funding and on designing an appropriate management and organisational structure.

Primed by key figures in the WECVS Steering Group, including those from James Pringle House, in July 1986 a proposal was developed and put forward to the BHA Management Board Meeting by the Director of Service Evaluation and Service Development, who was also the District Medical Officer (DMO). Speed was urged upon decision makers given the dangers of HIV transmission and "because of the involvement of the various voluntary agencies whose level of confidence in the NHS is somewhat fragile. It would at this stage be counter-productive to undermine the significant progress which has been somewhat painfully made with these groups" (Report to BHA Management Board Meeting, 1986).

This comment gives an insight into the tensions underlying the relationship between voluntary and statutory sectors, tensions which were later to have both a direct and profound influence on the development of the CLASH service.

In response to the proposal, a decision was made that subject to the availability of funds from the Regional Health Authority's (RHA) 1986/87 AIDS allocation, the Street Workers Project for AIDS should go forward. An immediate start on the project was planned, with funding for the remainder of the current financial year (1986/87) being drawn from the RHA's AIDS allocation, and with the expectation that funding for the following year might also be drawn from the same source. CLASH has since been funded by BHA through the Region's AIDS allocation, and supplemented since mid 1988 by special funds awarded by the Monument Trust[10] to BHA specifically for the purpose of developing HIV related community and care services.

The WECVS Steering Group produced an appropriate management structure (see Chapter Four), a title for the project - Central London Action on Street Health (CLASH), job descriptions for three outreach workers and advertisements for each of the posts in the *Guardian*, the *Voice*, and the *Pink Paper*. The WECVS Steering Group then planned to disband itself to be replaced by a Steering Group consisting of representatives from the voluntary sector and BHA. The three outreach workers, one man and two women, took up their posts in March 1987. One had experience of HIV and drugs related training and counselling, working with young people and working on the National AIDS Helpline, as well as some personal experience of drug use and of working as a prostitute; one had social work and counselling experience particularly in the field of drugs and HIV/AIDS; and the third had youth oriented detached work experience, although not exclusively with the client groups with which CLASH were to become involved.

Early development: Putting ideas into practice [1987-1988]

As an exercise in innovation and lacking models upon which to base its practice, the first six months of the project's history was an experimental period during which management and service practices were established. The first seven week induction period was spent equipping premises in the Soho Hospital[11], meeting with workers within BHA, the voluntary sector and key people involved in HIV service provision, attending relevant seminars and conferences, and beginning a period of attachment with the three voluntary agencies represented on the WECVS Steering Group - the Hungerford Drug Project, the Soho Project and the Basement Project. The placements lasted for three months, and included participation in one client drop-in session and one detached outreach session a week.

During this period, the workers were able to experience a variety of styles and methods of outreach and client based work, and familiarised themselves with a number of the locations where they were to undertake their own outreach work. The main disadvantage was that the clients contacted by CLASH were already in contact with services, particularly with the voluntary agencies with whom the team were on placement, and it soon became clear that the team needed to find other locations appropriate for their target groups and to develop their own working methods. The CLASH workers, once having received in-service training on specific skills and relevant health issues, felt able to begin exploring the possibility of undertaking their own HIV education and training with staff and clients from a variety of organisations working with their target groups.

At this time, arrangements were also made for supervision for individual team members and for external team consultancy. It was envisaged that supervision, provided at this point by the Principal Clinical Psychologist at JPH, was to be concerned with professional aspects of the work, while team consultancy, unusual in a statutory health service setting and provided by an external consultant once a week, was concerned with team dynamics and organisational practices, affording "a safe environment in which to express and explore the many pressures particular to our work" (CLASH, 1987).

There was an early recognition of the need to monitor the development and effectiveness of CLASH since the initiative was experimental in terms of service delivery, client groups and its unique voluntary-statutory collaboration. Negotiations had begun between the Department of Health, CLASH's Steering Group and Birkbeck College as to the feasibility of an evaluation of the CLASH project. In the meantime, the need for a flexible approach to allow the project to experiment in order to establish itself among target groups and to develop appropriate working practices was emphasised, particularly by voluntary representatives on the Steering Group with experience of similar work. As one voluntary manager explained:

"Working with any group of people in the street is an extremely time consuming process. Aside from the obvious preparatory work, constant further observational work in new possible working arenas must be undertaken... Most experienced detached workers would agree that there are no short cuts to providing a good street based service; and only a sound investment of time and 'foot-slogging', plus the necessity of office back up (which CLASH still sadly lack) will provide the proper basis" (Paper presented to Steering Group, 1987).

But while the voluntary representatives on the Steering Group were able to recognise the necessary requirements for the development and establishment of detached outreach work in general terms, they lacked experience in the specific aims and target groups of the CLASH service. As one voluntary manager indicates, they:

"had no direct knowledge of actually trying to impart health education on the street and what groups to target for instance... There was no way we could actually pinpoint that until workers were actually in the field and assessing the need and assessing the most appropriate avenues to actually pursue" (v).

Some representatives from the statutory sector accepted the argument that "it's actually very difficult to develop outreach work, and that a two year lead-in time is not unusual" (s), but doubts still remained about the fact that "it took an awfully long time to really get the confidence to do the outreach work required" and that "there didn't seem all that many contacts being made" (s). There was then, an uneasy ambivalence between attempting to recognise the difficult, "quite dangerous and quite frightening" nature of outreach work, and the desire for tangible results in terms of the numbers of clients being contacted (see Chapters Six and Seven). As part of the monitoring of progress and of the efficacy of working practices, and of the Steering Group's 'desire to know', it was requested that the CLASH team should provide a feedback report on their activities at each meeting of the Steering Group (six weekly intervals), and more extensive reviews upon request at periodic intervals.

After the initial six months, the CLASH team considered themselves to be in a position to clarify what had been accomplished and make proposals for the future direction of their work (CLASH, 1987). The questions to which the team addressed itself at this point were:

i.   what client group are we actually trying to contact?

ii. how are we going to make these contacts?

iii. what can we offer these clients once contact has been made?

On the first of these points, the team considered that the potential client group of young, vulnerable people was both large and amorphous, but that it was too soon to narrow their target groups too decisively. They felt they should continue to make contact with transient young people but also focus more particularly on drug users and workers in the sex industry. In accessing homeless young people, it was feared that the initial method of approach of making contacts through existing agencies whilst on placement, rendered them superfluous in terms of offering HIV advice and jeopardised their position as a separate entity with their own specific identity. They proposed to change their approach, and "to work peripatetically with hostels, night-shelters, day centres etc., where we would have a 'captive audience' of young people" (CLASH, 1987). They would undertake training work with staff of such organisations prior to working directly with the young people themselves. On the other hand, for the more focused work with drug users, the contact and presence on the scene already established by existing agencies would provide access to these groups. It was planned that a female CLASH worker would work one session a week with a detached worker from the Hungerford Drug Project. At this stage, the team had doubts about targeting rent boys, fearing that this might duplicate the work of existing agencies (e.g. the Soho Project). In order to access women prostitutes effectively, the team recognised that the use of direct and aggressive contacting strategies was necessary, and to facilitate this process, they proposed employing 'indigenous' sessional workers - that is workers with current or former experience of working as prostitutes.

The team were at this juncture concerned that they had nothing "concrete" to offer clients, while other community based agencies had for example, a drop-in or office based service. What they offered was their knowledge and skills in providing advice, counselling and referral.

Aware of their unique position spanning both statutory and voluntary services, the team felt they should develop their links with statutory services in two ways: first, to make services more accessible to their clients; and second, to influence the nature and style of statutory service provision in order to meet their clients' specific service needs. To facilitate referral into existing STD services at JPH, the team proposed establishing a coupon system, modelled on a similar system in New Jersey (Rhodes *et al.*, 1990a), through which referred clients could hand in a CLASH coupon on arrival for immediate appointments with particular sympathetic doctors and health advisors.

At this time, the team had also become concerned about their salary grading and levels of pay compared with other similar Health Service workers, such as those working at BHA's syringe exchange. In response to the team's concerns and proposals for service development, a paper produced by a voluntary sector representative of the Steering Group supported financial upgrading for the team, the use of indigenous sessional detached workers and a coupon or card system to facilitate referrals to key statutory services. In turn, the Steering Group endorsed each of the CLASH team's proposals (September-October, 1987), recommending that:

i.   a proposal for up-grading CLASH workers' pay levels should go forward to make them comparable with other similar Health Service workers;

ii. CLASH should continue to develop and undertake peripatetic outreach work with young people in hostels and other similar organisations working with the homeless, as well as people in prison, particularly Holloway Prison. CLASH should continue to balance training and peripatetic work with detached outreach work, and should consider assessing the relative value of each of these approaches as appropriate and effective uses of their time;

iii. CLASH should develop procedures to facilitate referral access for clients, while providing an assessment to District Steering Group of their clients' service needs, and the priority of referral to BHA services as opposed to services located elsewhere;

iv. CLASH should continue to target young people in need, but should also specifically target women and men working as prostitutes, drug users and drug injectors within this broad target group. CLASH should consider the relative value of a variety of contacting methods to reach these target groups, and these should include for example, advertising in contact magazines, and placing adverts and stickers in telephone boxes and at stations.

Development: Establishing practice [1988-1989]

Throughout the first half of 1988, CLASH continued to develop their outreach work as agreed with the Steering Group the previous year. Here we document the main developments in the team's detached, peripatetic and liaison work. More detailed discussions relating to the team's work, and its effectiveness in practice, are contained in later chapters.

Detached outreach work
Detached work with men working as prostitutes was developed in collaboration with the Soho Project, who had extensive experience of working in this area. At this stage, one session was undertaken every two weeks, with one male worker from each project. When contacted, rent boys were "given information about CLASH, free condoms" and an offer of appointments for more detailed advice and counselling in the CLASH office (CLASH, 1988). This office based service had started on a limited basis as an adjunct to providing referral to appropriate advice services, since it was found difficult to provide extensive counselling and advice in street settings. There were doubts about the appropriateness of encouraging office based counselling given the limited resources of CLASH.

Since no similar outreach work was established elsewhere in central London, CLASH were unable to facilitate the development of their outreach work with women prostitutes through collaboration. Initial work concentrated on contacting women prostitutes working from flats in and around Soho. After an initial blitz "knocking on every single door that had a red light or had a poster up" (w), the team developed a regular Thursday afternoon slot undertaken initially by three workers. Two female CLASH workers visited the flats, while a male worker from the Hungerford Drug Project remained outside to provide security. It was soon realised that it was unnecessary for the male worker to do this, and CLASH began to do this work alone. On first contact the workers aimed to introduce the services available, distributed a range of free condoms, determined whether the women required referral to existing health and advice services, and encouraged them to pass on information about CLASH to other working women. Eventually, relationships were established with a regular group of women prostitutes, who were provided with advice, condoms and referral. The team later varied the timing of their visits to widen the possibility of contacts.

As one of the workers indicated, at this point CLASH's "long-term aim was to work with women on the streets, transient women around King's Cross and so on" rather than to concentrate exclusively on contacting the more organised women prostitutes working from flats in Soho. This became possible once the team had established their outreach work in Soho and had gained in confidence and expertise. As with the Soho based work, work in King's Cross was to be initially undertaken in conjunction with a male worker from the Hungerford Drug Project and was equally, if not more, time consuming. Novel and aggressive methods of contact were required, some of which proved ineffective in practice, for example, advertisements in contact magazines, stickers placed in telephone boxes and an attempt to set up a telephone information and advice line (Moser and Lee, 1989). As outreach contacts began to be made in King's Cross, and as the work became established, the Steering Group "congratulated the team on this particular development, which can be widely represented as an innovative breakthrough in outreach work" (Steering Group Minutes, 1988). A more detailed description of the development of outreach work with women prostitutes is contained in an unpublished paper by two of the workers involved (Moser and Lee, 1989).

Detached work with drug users and drug injectors was developed through one detached outreach session a week in collaboration with a worker from the Hungerford Drug Project. Although initially slow to progress, largely because of intense police activity throughout the West End, collaboration with the Hungerford Project enabled CLASH to establish initial contact with drug users and to experience a variety of contacting and work methods.

Peripatetic outreach work
Peripatetic work with drug users involved a CLASH worker undertaking two sessions a week at the Hungerford Project syringe exchange. In addition, one CLASH worker undertook one afternoon session of group and individual work on health issues, while another undertook an evening session for women drug injectors at the BHA's syringe exchange in Cleveland Street. Peripatetic and collaborative work of this kind provided the team with invaluable opportunities to establish initial contact with drug-users and to gain a high profile within existing drug services in Bloomsbury and the voluntary sector.

Initial contacts had also been established with probation officers and health advisors in Holloway Prison with a view to establishing peripatetic work with women on remand for drug and soliciting offences. At this point, the work had yet to be fully negotiated or finalised.

Referral and liaison work
Liaison work with a range of projects and organisations was continuous throughout this period. This provided the CLASH workers with opportunities for further induction and for developing links with services to establish support networks and collaboration. CLASH themselves were also consulted about the aims and objectives of their outreach work by several voluntary agencies in London and further afield. In particular, firm links were established with Positively Women, a self-help group of women providing emotional and practical support to women with HIV infection, who were meeting regularly at the CLASH office, which enabled a variety of constructive contacts to be made. At this point, media contact, despite many invitations, was avoided.

The 'card system' designed to facilitate ease of referral access for clients was set up for use at JPH, Accident and Emergency, the Hungerford and Cleveland Street syringe exchange projects and at the Margaret Pyke Women's Health Centre. Referral links had also been established with the drug dependency unit (DDU) and GUMs at UCH, Rathbone Place[12], St. Stephens Hospital, St. Mary's Hospital and with a number of general practitioners working in Bloomsbury.

Moving on: A period of change [1989-1990]

During the next year the personnel of the CLASH team began to change. One of the women workers took study leave for a year to undertake a course in health education, leaving in mid-1988. She was replaced by a woman with experience of the sex industry and drug scenes, and ten years' voluntary sector experience largely working with young people, drug users and the homeless, but who had no direct experience of detached outreach work. The second woman from the original team left in December 1988, and a further male worker was recruited with a background in HIV community health promotion, gay and HIV voluntary work, and with some experience of youth detached work. At this stage there were plans to employ a sessional female worker who had experience of working as a prostitute, and although this plan proved inoperable, a woman sessional worker with professional experience of work in hostels, the voluntary sector and women's work was employed to work twenty hours a week from March 1989. She was regarded by

CLASH as a full team member working on a part-time basis. A second full-time woman worker who had experience of HIV related voluntary and training work, although again no direct experience of outreach work, began work in April 1989. The CLASH team at this point consisted of two full-time female workers, two full-time male workers and one part-time female worker.

The need to fill the administrative post, for which there had been partial funding in CLASH's original funding, was acknowledged by the Steering Group, but progress was painfully slow, and in November 1989 temporary secretarial help was arranged. In January 1990, a part-time administrator came into post. Just as the interests of the original team had shaped the early orientation of CLASH work, so the arrival of new workers created changes in focus for CLASH, and the expansion in size gave opportunities for expansion of services.

Detached outreach work
Work with rent boys and women prostitutes continued during the second year of the project, but a shift in emphasis occurred. Proportionately fewer rent boys and greater numbers of women prostitutes were contacted as the year progressed (see Chapter Six). Detached sessions at the Soho flats had increased to two afternoons a week and were staffed entirely by CLASH workers, as were the evening sessions at King's Cross, which had increased to three evenings a fortnight. Throughout this period CLASH had begun to formulate plans for furthering service delivery among rent boys and women prostitutes, which included proposals for establishing a mobile outreach unit and a women's drop-in and health centre based in King's Cross.

The CLASH team were expressing frustration in their work with drug-users - they were still largely operating through peripatetic work at BHA's and Hungerford's syringe exchange projects, but had begun to negotiate the possibilities for collaborative detached work (with the Hungerford Drug Project) in the Embankment area. The team had become critical of BHA's service provision for drug users, as had some voluntary agencies working in Bloomsbury. They were concerned about inflexible prescribing practices and insufficient and inadequate primary care facilities, which were considered to be a block on encouraging drug users to change risky behaviour. The team felt that the practical difficulties of accessing drug users through detached work was less of a problem than the lack of appropriate HIV related and care services on offer.

Peripatetic outreach work
Access to Holloway Prison was finally negotiated with the prison's education department, and CLASH's women workers regularly undertook discussion and training sessions both with women prisoners and prison officers. CLASH had also liaised with other agencies undertaking drugs and HIV related work in Holloway Prison, and were at this point hoping to negotiate additional access to the hospital wing. The team were planning similar work with male prisoners in Pentonville, but although access was gained and one initial session was undertaken, this work never became a regular commitment.[13] Throughout this period, a once weekly client drop-in service had been established at CLASH's premises, where clients were encouraged to drop-in for a chat, advice, information, counselling, condoms or syringe exchange.

Work with young people had concentrated on peripatetic outreach in existing hostel and homeless organisations, and the team had developed a range of 'learner centred' training packages tailored to the needs of the specific projects with which they worked. The team were, however, decreasing the amount of peripatetic training undertaken with young homeless people in favour of taking such work back out onto the street. They planned to network with other health education and training services in order to refer requests for such training to these organisations.

By late 1989, concern for the future of the CLASH project was emerging in the team and some of the voluntary representatives of the Steering Group, since funding was not secured beyond March 1990. Funding for the fourth CLASH worker (appointed in August 1988) had been provided from a grant by the Monument Trust to BHA for community and care developments in HIV related services. When approached for additional funding for CLASH in 1989, the Monument Trust requested clarification on some of the issues raised in the CLASH Bi-annual report, particularly those concerned with the extent and nature of outreach service provision. In response, an independent interim report to the Monument Trust was produced by the evaluation research team outlining the extent and nature of outreach contact with clients. To accompany this, the CLASH team produced their own response, concentrating on issues concerned with service delivery and service development.

In an attempt to make their case for funding to the Steering Group, the CLASH team produced a document outlining proposals for future service developments and initiatives for the six month period from September 1989 to March 1990 (CLASH, 1989). Apart from an impassioned plea for the continuation of the innovative work undertaken by the project, the proposals included:

i. improving management liaison between a designated person (the District AIDS Co-ordinator for example) and higher level health service management in order to facilitate the referral access of CLASH's clients into BHA services;

ii. development of the weekly drop-in service (which had been held up for the lack of a printed card advertising the service);

iii. development of a mobile outreach unit to be staffed by a health service doctor (from JPH), two nurses (from the Health Improvement Team) and two or three outreach workers;

iv. development of a low threshold drop-in and primary health centre for women prostitutes at King's Cross to enable immediate referral from outreach contacts (these two proposals were developed further in subsequent papers to the Steering Group);

v. development of prison work. At this point, access had been gained to Pentonville and work was soon to begin there, and hopes were high for a similar service in Brixton, although details had yet to be negotiated;

vi. production of further accessible health education materials;

vii. expansion of the work with rent boys once more, since service provision had fallen behind that of other target groups, largely because one of the two workers responsible had withdrawn from detached outreach work (see Chapter Six).

Concerned about tardy future funding provision, two voluntary representatives of the Steering Group commended the work of CLASH. One stated that the project had achieved "work that has come to be seen as good and innovative by a broad range of other street agencies, with a difficult and very transient client group" (Letter to Steering Group, 1989). The other argued that "there should be a three year plan to develop the project since CLASH's work had been seen as good and innovative by voluntary organisations and although it was recognised that there had been some management problems with the project" it was "essential for Bloomsbury to maintain its credibility in dealing with issues around HIV/AIDS by retaining and supporting its outreach work" (Steering Group Minutes, 1989).

In response, the CLASH Steering Group recommended that a proposal for a further three years' funding should be prepared by CLASH and the District AIDS Co-ordinator. The proposal was to be put forward to the District AIDS Steering Group (September, 1989). At the recommendation of the CLASH Steering Group, this should include a proposal for an external consultant to review the work of CLASH and identify the direction the project should take over the three year period, paying particular attention to policy development and management issues. The decision to commission management consultancy had been agreed by the Chair of the Steering Group and a representative of the Monument Trust, who were deliberating on whether to continue to fund CLASH. Once the management consultancy had been arranged, within two months both BHA's District AIDS Steering Group and the Monument Trust agreed to fund the project for a further two years, with funding for a third year dependent upon the outcome of the management consultancy and its implications in practice (Steering Group Minutes, 1989). The CLASH project was then funded at least until March 1992.

Although funding had been secured, there was concern from the CLASH team and some voluntary representatives as to the exact role of the management consultant. First, although the terms of reference suggested that the consultant was to take on an advocacy role on behalf of the CLASH team, it was at times unclear as to whether this was to be the case since the consultancy had clearly been suggested and invited at the request of only selected (statutory) members of the Steering Group. Second, there was the question of whether the Department of Health funded evaluation (of which this report forms a part) would duplicate the consultant's input, and would provide a more depth account of the management problems, producing a firmer foundation for recommendations. The fundamental purpose of inviting management consultancy, however, was to ensure a critical review of the problems and inadequacies of management prior to the securing of funding.

The terms of reference outlined two areas which the Steering Group wished the consultant to address (Steering Group Minutes, 1989; Letter to consultant, 1990): first, he was to assess the management structure in relation to the goals of CLASH and make recommendations for future management; and second, he was to consider the interaction between voluntary and statutory sectors in the functioning of CLASH. The consultant was to undertake this work "on behalf of CLASH and the Steering Group", and was to collaborate closely both with the CLASH team and the evaluation research team.

The consultant conducted his enquiries between June and July the following year, and reported to the Steering Group in September 1990. In principle, the consultant's recommendations involved the appointment of a CLASH Team Co-ordinator who should act as the team's line manager, accountable to BHA's HIV Prevention Co-ordinator, who in turn would be accountable to the District AIDS Co-ordinator; and for the Steering and Management Groups to be replaced by an Advisory Group with both voluntary and statutory input but with little or no decision-making or management power. The recommendations thus brought CLASH in line with the hierarchy of NHS management, and diluted the statutory-voluntary management partnership which had formed the Steering Group (see Chapter Five).

Throughout the period during which funding was secured and the consultancy took place (September 1989-July 1990), the CLASH team's work progressed relatively slowly along the lines of their proposals presented to the Steering Group the previous August. At the request of the Steering Group the team put forward revised and more detailed proposals for the development of the mobile outreach unit and the low threshold women's drop-in and health centre. At the recommendation of the Steering Group, these were referred to the Management Group for detailed discussion and consideration. At the point of completing data collection (September, 1990) there had been little further progress, though in early 1991, with the encouragement of a selection of interested doctors and health advisors at JPH (and to a lesser degree of those on CLASH's Steering and Management Groups), plans were going ahead to further structure the proposals and to gain a suitable premises near King's Cross for the women's drop-in and health centre. Plans were also in progress to establish a weekly satellite STD clinic at the CLASH office, to be staffed by JPH doctors, for clients attending the client drop-in service.

Since the consultancy has been completed, the CLASH team has gone through a further series of staff changes. A new male worker with experience of HIV voluntary work, although with no experience of detached or outreach work, was appointed in August to replace a male worker who left in February. In the intervening period before the male worker was replaced, CLASH employed a male locum worker for three months to undertake office based client and administrative work. Additional sessional workers were also recruited: in May 1990, a female worker with experience of prison work to undertake detached work with women prostitutes; in the same month the evaluator began street detached work/participant observation with rent boys. Shortly after the consultancy had been completed, a further female worker left, and the remaining member of the original CLASH team, who had been with CLASH for three years, announced his resignation (partly in response to the recommendations made by the consultant; see following Chapter). In early 1991, the CLASH team consisted of two full-time workers, one female (with two and a half years CLASH experience) and one male (with six months CLASH experience), one full-time administrator, and three sessional workers. CLASH still awaited the appointment of two further full-time workers (one female, one male), following the departure of their predecessors in May and August respectively, since at the recommendation of the Steering Group it was decided not to appoint replacements until the consultant's recommendations were in operation.

CLASH was poised at a point of change. And as the following chapters outline, the implications for the project's management and service functioning may have been radically altered as a result of the management consultant's recommendations.

"My summing up is that I think CLASH is and could be a really good project, but I think it still is in it's development stage of sorting it out. And I think there needs to be drastic changes and I think those will bring along the improvements with it" (w).

CHAPTER FOUR

MANAGEMENT STRUCTURE AND FUNCTIONING

The increased commitment to community based approaches to health education and service provision has encouraged a concomitant tendency for intersectoral collaboration. This has characterised much of the recent history of community development for health, although the potential for collaboration from a diversity of service perspectives and the commitment to developing community-based intervention has been heightened by the advent of HIV infection and AIDS. Approaches to outreach intervention, despite historically remaining closer to health initiatives developed from within affected communities themselves, are not immune to this process. In the United States, the organisation and practice of outreach intervention from a combination of 'community' and 'professional' service perspectives is not uncommon, and in the United kingdom is increasing.

In this chapter we describe the management structure of the CLASH project and its functioning in practice. It too involves collaboration - between statutory and voluntary health sectors. At the time of implementation (early 1987), not only were there few interventions devoted specifically to HIV related outreach work in the United Kingdom, there were none to our knowledge which employed such a unique model of management. These aims of integrating voluntary and statutory health sector service provision meant structuring the unique model of outreach management which we describe here. As becomes clear from the views and expectations of those involved, both sides in the collaboration were "in uncharted waters", with no models of appropriate organisational structure to follow, and with little idea of how best to collaborate. Both groups were convinced that there was a need for the CLASH intervention and that this was to be best achieved through collaboration.

Emergence and establishment of management structure

The WECVS Steering Group had in May 1986 suggested a simple management structure to consist of a management committee working directly with the intended three outreach workers. This committee was to consist of six to twelve managers with equal representation from both statutory and voluntary sectors. Members were to be chosen on the basis of their expertise in the work areas relevant to the CLASH project: detached outreach, training and education, drugs work, clinical practice, and health service management and administration. It was envisaged that the group should meet once every month, if not, at least every six weeks, with a sub-group meeting more frequently for day to day supervision and support. The objectives of this group were to:

> "enable workers to carry out their work brief. It should be involved in deciding aims and objectives and assist the workers to prioritise their workload. Policy decisions, financing and the concern for the workers welfare and employment conditions should all be functions of the committee" (Document to WECVS Steering Group, 1986)

In further meetings this structure was subsequently abandoned in favour of one which was more elaborate, and by October, it was agreed that in principle the CLASH team would be managed by BHA's Community Unit, District Health Education Officer and Clinical Psychologist. The Community Unit was accountable to the Community Unit General Manager (CUGM), and a line manager was to be designated by the CUGM to be responsible for the team's terms of employment, administrative matters and day-to-day management. The District Health Education Officer and Clinical Psychologist would be responsible for 'professional' management including "project work, teaching skills, health education, clinical aspects of training, links with James Pringle House, planning materials, etc." (Document to WECVS Steering Group, 1986).

It was proposed that the WECVS Steering Group should continue to meet monthly until the project was established. At that point it should become a Management Group as defined above. The transition from Steering to Management Group, however, never occurred. Rather, the Steering Group remained in place with the Community Unit General Manager as Chair, while it was decided that in addition there was to be a Management Group responsible for the day-to-day running of the project, administration, and professional guidance and support for the workers. Thus the WECVS Steering Group consisting of statutory and voluntary representatives remained as Steering Group, and a representative from BHA's Community Unit, BHA's District Health

Education Officer and Clinical Psychologist became the Management Group.

The structure, membership and function of the Steering Group has also been subject to change and development over time. The first formal meeting of CLASH's Steering Group (16 April, 1987) agreed that a distinction be drawn between the role of the Steering Group and the management of the project and that terms of reference should be drawn up accordingly. These terms of reference emerged in December 1987, when the project had been in operation for nine months, and were finalised by March 1988.

The final version of the terms of reference laid out the requirement of the CLASH Steering Group to determine strategy, policy and practice for CLASH within the framework of DHA policy and in consultation with the CLASH team; to reflect the joint interest of the DHA and local non-statutory groups in limiting the spread of HIV infection in central London and, therefore, to provide a balanced representation of statutory and voluntary representatives to facilitate mutually beneficial links between both sectors. As far as operational management was concerned, the CLASH team were to be accountable to the Unit General Manager, Community and Dental Services Unit, Local and Community Services Division, BHA. For day to day management the team were to report to the Associate Unit General Manager. The Management Group was to meet by arrangement and consisted of the Associate Unit General Manager (for administrative matters); a Clinical Psychologist from James Pringle House (clinical matters); and the District Health Education Officer (health education). This was to provide the types of management with which the Health Service was familiar - administrative and professional.

A link into District AIDS services was provided by the dual presence of members of the Steering Group on the District AIDS Steering Group (DASG), responsible for District policy formation and service direction. The Unit General Manager (UGM) and the District AIDS Co-ordinator were to represent the work of the CLASH team and Steering Group on the DASG. The UGM also chaired the AIDS Community Policy Group which was to "ensure consistency in policy and practice between non-acute AIDS services" which included the Community and Dental Services Unit, Mental Health Unit, syringe exchange, DDU, JPH, Terminal Care Support and health advisors (CLASH Team's Terms of Reference, 1987).

Management in practice: Collaboration and conflict

The resulting management structure is represented in the figure below (Figure 4.1). The Steering Group (where the CLASH workers were 'in attendance') consisted of representatives from BHA involved in health education, health promotion, public health, HIV service co-ordination, Health Authority management and HIV related social and epidemiological research, and representatives from the voluntary sector involved in street detached work, youth advice work with young people, the homeless, drug users and male prostitutes and people with concerns about HIV infection and AIDS. Balanced on the one hand by the Management Group, which was exclusively statutory in representation, it was balanced on the other by a Voluntary Sub-Group. This group emerged in response to tensions developing between outreach workers and statutory managers, at the request of the CLASH team. It was exclusively voluntary, and aimed to provide support and direction on issues directly associated with the development of appropriate service provision and outreach working practice.

Figure 4.1, however, is an ideal representation of the functioning of the management structure. The Management Group, when it did give administrative direction, rarely provided the CLASH team with the professional supervision intended. The Voluntary Sub-Group survived for a year and then disappeared: "That group is not meeting now, it was not very powerful, it was basically struck down with a case of apathy" (w). Similarly, voluntary sector representation on the Steering Group began to decline during 1989, and by early 1990 was almost entirely absent, although later revived. Throughout this latter period, some voluntary participants influential in initiating the CLASH intervention did not appear at all. Statutory representation was also variable, and throughout the early months of 1990 it was not uncommon for the Steering Group to consist of the Chair and two or three statutory representatives with the CLASH team in attendance. As a result, the principle of collaboration behind the Steering Group's decision making process became difficult to achieve in practice.

The evaluation identified four main factors which appeared to contribute to the lack of co-ordination and integration in management functioning: the structure and orientation of the CLASH team; conflict in worker-manager relations; issues of ideology and power in statutory-voluntary relations; and participants' changing interests and levels of involvement. Each of these are examined below.

Figure 4.1 Management and service structure and function

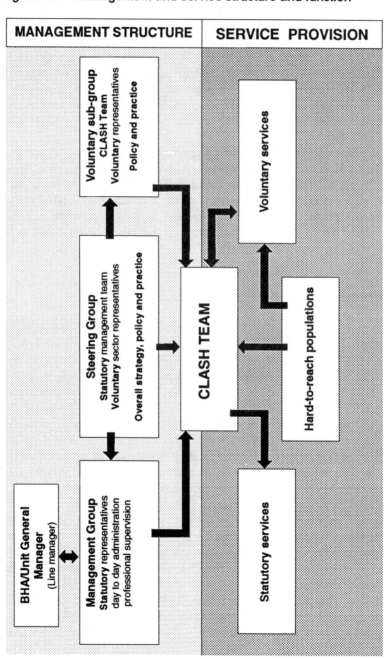

These four factors can be viewed in the context of an initial polarisation of interest, particularly between outreach workers and statutory managers, where two groups inhabiting entirely alien cultures confronted each other in mutual incomprehension. Throughout this initial period neither made constructive attempts to 'bridge gaps' and any principles of 'collaboration' were temporarily lost. Statutory managers' images of the CLASH team as wilful children refusing to understand the awesome but necessary realities of NHS bureaucracy were exacerbated in practice by the team's tendency to "stamp [their] feet to get what [they] wanted" (w).

Over time and as familiarity was gained, compromises and adjustments were made, but not before considerable misunderstanding, exasperation and paranoia had been generated. While differences in perception, orientation and ideology between participants may have contributed to the problems of organisation and management at the core of the CLASH initiative, the fundamental problem was structural, embedded in the forms of organisation adopted.

The structure and orientation of the CLASH team

The members of the CLASH team were employed as three individual workers with identical job descriptions, although clearly each brought particular and different skills to the job. The team had been established with no specification of internal structures of team management and organisation. In the vacuum of non-direction, the workers themselves made the decision to operate as a collective. This meant that each had equal involvement in the internal organisation, management and decision making processes within the team. Their commitment to working as a collective was strong, and generated a clear corporate identity within the team. This coloured both their approach to work issues within the team as well as having direct effects on the nature and style of their relations with the Steering and Management Groups.

As far as management functioning was concerned, the problem centred on the viability of a collective operating within a host organisation firmly rooted in hierarchical management structures. The Health Authority had never before experienced this style of management, and in the early stages there was little conception of how the collective might function in practice. The potential for problems in this unusual mix of conflicting management styles was intensified by the fact that the style and nature of outreach work, and the orientation of the outreach workers themselves, were closer to voluntary and community-oriented approaches which are more likely to operate on egalitarian or democratic principles. In essence, the relation between the CLASH team, as a collective, and the Health Authority, as institutional hierarchy, provided an insight into, and a paradigmatic instance of, the nature of the collaboration itself: a window into the mix of styles and ideologies which formed the collaboration between 'community' and 'professional' service responses. Even in these very early days of management, the foundations for conflict between workers and managers, and between voluntary and statutory representatives on the Steering Group were in place, resulting from the structures of management adopted and the divergence of approaches that these encouraged between the CLASH team and the Steering Group. As recognised by one statutory manager:

"They [CLASH] are more aligned to non-statutory sector services yet being managed within the statutory service. The very nature of the people that one wants to recruit into jobs like that makes them less amenable to the bureaucracy that the health service actually chucks out" (s).

There was general consensus among both voluntary and statutory representatives that the team's decision to work as a collective occurred in the absence of direction from management. The CLASH team was simply established with three workers in post, each with identical job descriptions, each with equal status in terms of seniority of position and salary, and with no provisions made for a senior worker or team leader. In many ways, as indicated by two voluntary managers, the irony was that the Health Authority had created a collective before the outreach workers were in post:

"Perhaps the workers are victims of inadequate management in the first place. [But for the workers] there were not any options, no one was in charge. There wasn't a hierarchical structure to start with, so they didn't have any choice, they *were* a collective" (v).

"In some ways that was kind of accidental... so that was maybe a fault, the fact that it wasn't really addressed" (v).

One statutory manager tended to view this as the first error in the management process:

"Yes it was their [CLASH's] decision. I think originally we appointed three people on the same grade and that was probably an error" (s).

As a collective, the team "presented a corporate image", required a group decision on almost every issue, and often "came round as a threesome" when approaching project managers (s). This was seen as inhibiting the management process and the flow of decision making by some managers:

"It got to the point where it became a bit of a joke where you couldn't talk about seeing a member of the CLASH team. You had to see the whole CLASH team" (s).

This 'team approach' meant that the CLASH team were able to protect themselves by acting as a solidary unit against the Health Authority, but over time it became clear that the apparent consensus of 'collective' working masked a reality of divided opinion and conflict within the team. In interviews, several statutory participants mentioned differences between the collective decisions of the team and the voiced opinions of individual members in private discussion. These tensions also became apparent in interviews with individual team members, and were reflected in their often colourful descriptions of collective working: "the tyranny of collective working"; "an unequal collective"; "the hidden hierarchy of the collective" (w).

The unequal power relations operating within the team, and their consequences for the disruption of collective intra-team management and functioning were a function of two inter-related factors: the differing power relations operating between individuals on the basis of personality, work experience and expertise; and the problematic functioning of the team's lengthy decision making process. In this way, the weekly team review meetings (where observations were regularly undertaken), which often lasted a whole day, and where collective team decisions were made, became a battlefield for the tensions and conflicts existing between individual team members.

Within a team with an unusually high turnover of staff, individual team members' level of experience and expertise was rarely considered 'equal'. Although not necessarily a reason to create problems in team functioning, this, coupled with distinctive personality clashes within the team, and the perceptions of outreach work as demanding 'street-cred' workers with certain 'qualifications' in terms of life-experience and 'attitude', became a source of conflict, where workers would often wrangle for the recognition of power and control within the team. This process, although rarely overt, meant that workers new to post, or without the 'acceptable' background, often experienced the practice of collective working as illusory. As one of the more recent appointments to the team indicated, long-standing team members found it:

> "hard to let go of that power... it's not really fair for the other team members that come along, because it means that they never get the chance to be equal, because there's this hidden hierarchy" (w).

The clashes between team members which ensued, although often viewed in terms of differences in 'personality', were equally rooted in the power differences operating between workers, and rendered collective decision making almost impossible:

> "I basically felt like there was a real power struggle going on. A power struggle that I didn't really want to be part of. But I couldn't help being involved in it because if I didn't then what was happening was rather than keeping my position... I would just go under because I would have things pushed on me. And so I felt that I had to fight" (w).

Beyond the problems of power and control in decision making and their implications for the working of the team as a collective - to which we return below, the problems in intra-team functioning may also have been encouraged by the size of the team. Several statutory participants felt a team of three would inevitably prove to be problematic:

> "Amongst three people you'll get two versus one, or you'll get one personality stronger than the other two. I watched for signs of emerging actual leadership and they appeared occasionally... I felt that I needed to hang onto my own assessment of what I thought their collective was about, as well as what they presented. A team isn't constructed on paper or it isn't constructed of equal grades. In the Health Service we know about teamwork; they might not be equal but there are still teams, and teams are dominated either by a traditional profession, or they're distorted from that traditional model by particular circumstances. You just

watch particular circumstances, and I was just watching for what might emerge from that one" (s).

In this sense, the conflicts between individual workers for control and ownership of particular aspects of the team's work may have arisen in part through the naturally occurring 'leadership' qualities of particular workers. This too, need not necessarily render the functioning of a collective problematic, although in the context of CLASH where the collective appeared to be based - quite simply and perhaps naively - on 'equality' throughout, this may have added to workers' already deeply rooted frustrations.

In this context, the team's weekly decision making meetings functioned very precariously indeed. Much of the process of actually making decisions was plagued by lengthy discussion - sometimes heated arguments - over the 'role' of particular workers in relation to particular aspects of the work. Each of the workers became responsible for specific work remits, and each in turn became defensive of their individual work interests and positions within the team. Rather than functioning as a team, CLASH functioned as disparate individuals, and decisions affecting the whole team would rarely be made without argument or voiced disagreement. Workers who disagreed with decisions would either ignore them when it came to action or be persistent in re-presenting them on agendas week after week. Since the team was nonetheless concerned to protect the *idea* of collective working, agenda items or decisions were often deferred until all team members were present - a rare event, and a process which meant decisions were sometimes deferred for weeks. As one of the workers remarked: "we managed ourselves very badly. I think its improving, but I think it's appalling" (w).

Central to the team's management functioning was the problem of accountability and responsibility. As one worker commented of another:

"He wasn't actually accountable to anyone. He was accountable to all of us, but in that also he was accountable to none of us" (w).

One particularly potent example of this process, was when, for a combination of emotional and personal reasons, one of the male workers withdrew from undertaking detached outreach work. As a consequence, the flow of detached work with rent boys was disrupted and the numbers of new contacts dropped severely (see Chapter Six). In response, the team took it upon themselves to give the worker a three month deadline, by which time he had to make a decision either to continue with detached work or to resign from the project. It was not until the worker chose to resign, however, that either the Steering or Management Group were informed. Over a management issue of some importance - where in effect a worker was not fulfilling his terms of employment - the team, protected by the notion of collective working, felt confident to manage themselves, remaining both independent from, and unaccountable to, the appropriate lines of management. As one of the workers said of this event: "to go to management... would be seen as such a gross act of betrayal, that no-one would... I would see no-one daring to do it" (w).

Managers acknowledged the problem of responsibility and accountability as far as liaison between the team, Steering and Management Groups were concerned:

> "On one level they're autonomous and another level they're not, and it's not clear to people always to whom they're responsible" (s).

> "Here was a group of people who said 'we're all equal, none of us is the leader, and we don't report to anybody" (s).

The fact that the team had "a fair degree of independence, which they wanted to maintain" was. therefore, viewed as "creating difficulties" (s). One other statutory manager, comparing CLASH with other professional groups within the Health Service, saw the project as lacking in accountability, precisely because of their organisational and management structure:

> "I don't think they are any more or less constrained than any other professional group, but perhaps by having these cumbersome structures of management committees and steering committees they appear to be accountable. In reality I don't think they are" (s).

Gradually emerging within the team, however, was a desire for direction and accountability, although this was rarely vocalised between team members as fervently as were the team's collective ideals:

"We didn't feel contained and held in any sort of structure, and that's why we desperately built up a whole lot of structures around us. Like all these sub-groups, like an attempt to hook ourselves into something, and actually to be accountable" (w).

Long before this stage, in an attempt to improve the internal functioning of the project, the team were meeting weekly with an external consultant. The aim was for the team to explore group dynamics and intra-team relations in order "to formulate new ways of working together" (w):

"What we managed to do over a long process in consultancy was identify structures and identify means of getting what we need in terms of structures, goals and timing" (w).

Although the team found the consultancy constructive, the process was slow, and evidence of improvement in management functioning as a result was slim. Even to sympathetic statutory managers such consultancy remained an entirely alien concept:

"All this jargon would come out, 'I need to know that I can talk to people about my troubles, counselling, team-building' - it was a different world from the increasingly ruthless world of general management, and seemed terribly precious" (s).

The need in practice for systematic direction and accountability to improve intra-team functioning led ultimately to a desire for explicit hierarchy. This appeared, however, to be as much a concern about the unwieldy and time consuming processes involved in actually arriving at mutually agreeable decisions, as it was a concern of the more experienced workers to have overt recognition of their position and power within the team: "I certainly didn't want to be anything other than a team member before, but I feel differently now" (w). Two of the longer standing CLASH workers in particular, put forward their suggestions that there should be two senior posts created within the team. As one of them outlined: a director "dealing with the policies and structures and the direct liaison with management" and a practice co-ordinator "dealing with the development of the actual work and the staff supervision" (w). Other team members, however, felt that the only effective way to create a leadership or co-ordinating post within the team was to make an external appointment.

Most statutory and voluntary managers had felt the need for re-structuring the team hierarchically for a considerable time, indeed that it was an error that the team had been allowed to develop as a collective. By the time that most were aware that problems of intra-team management existed - though they had never been overtly communicated between workers and managers - and at the request of the Steering group, a management consultant was appointed to collaborate with the team in clarifying a hierarchical structure. By Autumn 1990, the team and Steering Group had accepted the consultant's proposal that an external appointment should be made to a co-ordinating, managerial post within the CLASH team. This person would act as line manager and professional supervisor to outreach workers, be responsible for liaising with the Health Authority, co-ordinate the direction of CLASH's outreach work, and would be accountable to the Health Authority's HIV Prevention Co-ordinator.

In this way, the outreach workers were actively involved in replacing their once protected 'collective' with the form of management to which they had been forcefully opposed. But precisely how much the team's commitment to collective working and opposition to hierarchy was a function of democratic principle rather than of survival (as they perceived it) in an alien host organisation with alien management and work cultures is difficult to determine. Similarly, it appears likely that the team's swing from the ideals of collective working towards a team hierarchy was both a function of the more powerful workers wishing to have their power endorsed, as well as the less powerful workers wishing to prevent their marginalisation in the existing "hidden hierarchy". In this respect, it is significant that one of the workers who had proposed that the appointment be made internally within CLASH, resigned shortly after the Steering Group had endorsed the consultant's recommendations.

In principle then, having been made directly accountable to a team co-ordinator and in turn to the Health Authority, the CLASH team (at the time of writing) have been positioned further within the NHS hierarchy (see Chapter Five). This may result in a loss of the team's rather unusual autonomy and independence to decide upon intra-team working and management practices themselves. Rather, they are to be imposed from above, through a hierarchical system of NHS line managers, who are ultimately accountable (as was the Steering Group) to the Health Authority's Unit General Manager.

Reverting to a hierarchical system of team management may have appeared the simple way both for the workers to resolve the problems of collective intra-team management and for the Health Authority to gain some control over a team which often appeared to mobilise collectively simply in order to protect its autonomy and independence (see Chapter Five). There was a clear need to re-organise the internal management structure of the team, and constructing a hierarchicy was one solution. But the CLASH workers were not totally disillusioned with collectives - or a non-hierarchical task-oriented style of management - considering this a feasible management option given the appropriate structures, direction and support:

> "I think a collective could still work in a sense of if we were honest about our power positions then we'd devolve that onto less experienced people" (w).

> "If you have a collective where you all have a task, a task designation kind of collective, that's going to work better than if you have a collective where everyone mucks in and everyone's doing everything or nothing" (w).

Worker-management relations: Conflict in identity and practice

Tensions between outreach workers and statutory managers were perhaps inevitable in a collaboration of this type. Although part of its 'innovative' charm, these tensions stemmed from a relatively natural collusion between the CLASH workers and the voluntary representatives on the basis of shared experience, conceptualisations of health and service provision and ideological positioning. In the face of perceptions of the Health Service as clumsy and inadequate in providing for hard-to-reach clients' needs, this alliance often became a defensive one, remaining protective - sometimes even paternalistic - towards clients. Inadequacies in statutory sector performance were therefore expected *a priori*, even if at times they were not always evident. In practice, this meant that outreach workers were placed in a situation where their identity as outreach workers was continuously under challenge and often confused between the reality and experience of being statutory employees and their individual identities as community workers. Once again, the experiences of collaboration for the workers and managers involved gives a useful insight into the far reaching consequences of what it actually meant for the Health Authority to collaborate in this way. The battle which ensued between workers and statutory managers was about identity and ownership of the work:

"If the voluntary organisation had more power, the job that the voluntary organisations do is very similar to what we do, OK we're like a voluntary project, except we're statutory, so we wouldn't have to fight with them about what we want, because they already know what we want, because they're doing it in their projects, right? It's the statutory that we're fighting, and that's why it's so difficult" (w).

In this context, worker-statutory manager relations became polarised, and participants would attend Steering Group meetings expecting the latest in a series of confrontations:

"The Steering Group became confrontational. And I have a very clear view that members of the voluntary sector and the CLASH group actually got together before the steering committee to say, 'OK, what do we need to get out of this today"... The Steering Group was bizarre. It was confrontational, it was always 'what does management feel?' " (v).

"The Group's actual survival... was hinging on whether we could hold a steering meeting together without people walking out, and that was a very real danger... you know, people saying 'I really do not know what the point of these meetings are; they're hostile, they're aggressive, we don't make decisions, the Health Authority side is suspicious and grossly cautious of everything'. You need quite sophisticated input to keep that going" (s).

In some ways the management structure of CLASH resembled a management structure from the voluntary sector: they had 'managers' who were volunteers rather than employed for the task, whose power was unspecified and limited, and whose time input could not be completely relied upon. And they experienced almost the worst of those aspects of voluntary sector management, despite also having very strong support for their work and working alongside some of the voluntary managers on the development of outreach work. This very support and ideological similarity led to the voluntary-statutory sector split, in which CLASH aligned themselves with the voluntary sector. The Voluntary Sub-Group was set up to provide a separate arena in which proposals and policies could be worked through by voluntary sector representatives and the CLASH team before exposure to Steering Group and statutory sector management:

"If we've got certain things we want to say, and we'd like something to happen... we'll tell the voluntary staff so they can argue it for us at the Steering Group, because otherwise, it would be just CLASH with the management" (w).

For the outreach workers the voluntary participants became go-betweens, close allies who would help them to get what they wanted from the 'management' - perceived as exclusively statutory in orientation, even if not in membership. As one of the members of the Voluntary Sub-Group commented: "they'd come in and bitch about the Management Group... it was very much them and us" (v). For some statutory managers, as is clear from the quote given earlier, this was viewed as confrontational: *they were* being set up.

There was a general feeling that the unwieldy management structure and the tensions between collective and hierarchical elements left CLASH both mis-managed at the day-to-day team level and under-managed at the Steering and Management Group level.

"Basically we get no managerial supervision at all. Not that I particularly would want managerial supervision, but it's not even offered. We get no clinical supervision provided by the Health Authority either" (w).

"We're managed by the statutory but we don't really get much management, we don't get much encouragement, nobody's coming to us helping us - we're having to go up to them and tell them what we want, and then fight with them to get what we want, and then wait a long time to see if anything occurs" (w).

This was as much to do with the practical problems of management as it was to do with how to supervise these "weird creatures" called outreach workers. The professional and clinical supervision for the CLASH workers promised by the Management Group rarely materialised:

"With a group like CLASH it's very unclear what their professional management should be, because there is no obvious animal. I mean, if you have health advisors there's a health advisor hierarchy, in our case a psychologist with some kind of overall charge of the direction of things - but for a group like this there is no obvious line management to fit in" (s).

Similarly, problems in everyday management were exacerbated by the team's lack of expertise in dealing with NHS styles of management, their "levels of resentment of managerial interference", and the Health Authority's difficulty in managing a team so "unusual" (s). There are many examples of instances in the administrative process which became the source for conflict between workers and managers, and an incredible amount of management time was spent in extreme, and probably unnecessary, disagreement. Here we briefly cite two examples. The first, which occurred early on in the project's history, and which soon became a symbolic landmark to illustrate the project's "management cultural difference" (s), involved the acquisition of furniture and office equipment for the project's premises. Having been appointed with virtually no Health Service management experience or training, the team simply bought the equipment they required and presented the Management Group with a receipt. As the Unit General Manager and Chair of the Steering Group at the time explains, this was both to do with the team's lack of NHS experience and urge to 'test the boundaries':

"They went off and bought furniture and cups and saucers and tea-towels and mugs and whatever from Habitat... and then arrived and presented us with a bill for it... At my level of seniority in the organisation, earning the kind of money that I do, with a staff of 1600 people, I can't go to Habitat and buy furniture and bring in a bill. Now you can attribute some of that to naivety, but you can also attribute it to exactly what happens to small children... I still think its something like the average five year old where they're pushing the frontiers to see how far they can push the organisation" (s).

And as the manager above indicated, precisely because the CLASH team were considered so unusual, they found ways to go on 'pushing the organisation':

"At some point one has to say well 'hang on, within this service this is where the ring fence goes. You can't step out of that without having you're knuckles rapped'. Now alright, because they were new and unusual, we found ways of satisfying the auditors... any other staff group that behaved like that would have faced disciplinary action. They didn't" (s).

While this might in retrospect seem quite comic, it highlights the practical difficulties experienced in the management of the project. Having employed community workers without the necessary experience to deal with NHS management, the team - safe in its guise of the collective - remained slow to learn. This was in part because the team had received little appropriate induction and in part because they were unwilling to be inducted. It was also a result of the team's unwillingness to accept NHS procedures since these were seen as inhibiting the functioning of project work. There is an element of truth in this latter point, as one further example illustrates.

Adequate staffing remains critical to maintaining the continuity of project work. This is particularly the case with outreach work, as teams often work in pairs to ensure the safety of workers and clients. Despite these most basic requirements, the CLASH team suffered relentless problems with the Health Authority in attempting to arrange the employment of project workers. This was particularly the case regarding the employment of black workers, which CLASH saw as critical to the composition of the team. This resulted in lengthy disputes between the CLASH team and statutory personnel about the precise wording of job adverts and about established NHS employment procedure:

"There was this whole big shenanigan about having to have a black women worker, which we [statutory managers] all supported in principle, but actually the Health Authority being an equal opportunities employer needed to be able to demonstrate that it wasn't throwing its own equal opportunities policy in the bin. In the end that was satisfactorily resolved, but CLASH needed to do their side in the deal as well" (s).

Similarly, despite having partial funding in the original budget, and despite continually being acknowledged as long overdue by members of the Steering Group, the employment of the team's administrator took some 20 months, while two full-time posts which became vacant in May and August 1990 respectively had yet to be filled some eight months later, and appointments were not to be made until the project's team co-ordinator came into post (summer 1991). While this process had admittedly has been hampered by disagreement between the team, the Steering Group and the Management Group as to the precise contractual arrangements of the posts, this had direct and negative consequences on the team's capacity to function effectively. At the time of writing, without half its full-time work force, much of CLASH's detached work, most of which was conducted in pairs of workers of the same gender, was forced to rely almost entirely on collaborative work with neighbouring projects and sessional workers to function at all.

Despite the problems encountered in the management of the project, it was not for the want of trying. Paradoxically the CLASH project received a singular and disproportionate amount of high level Health Service management time. While representing a small proportion of those managed by the Health Authority, and a tiny proportion of the budget, the CLASH team were managed, even on a day-to-day level, by extremely senior staff (for example, BHA's Unit General Manager sat on both the Steering and the Management Groups):

"CLASH was actually taking a disproportionately large chunk of management time. This amazing kind of support system from the senior management of the District for three workers, whereas if you take community nursing, there are 317 I think... they have a director of nursing services who would see [the UGM] for about half an hour a week. There are 317 staff being managed by that amount of time! That's the standard tradition of Health Service management structure... CLASH was unusual. We all went along with it because it didn't fit anywhere else" (s).

So without pre-existing models of management practice for the Health Authority to follow, and in the context of having to 'do something', the management of CLASH demanded the attention of those otherwise concerned with senior management. The senior manager's remark above that "we all went along with it because it didn't fit in anywhere else" appears particularly apposite. Similarly, when CLASH had built itself as a collective, the Health Authority sat at a distance, 'going along with it', with little idea about 'what to do'. And just as here the Health Authority eventually saw its lack of foresight and subsequent inaction as regrettable, managers soon began to wonder precisely what was being achieved by the involvement of particularly senior members of Health Service staff. Their frustration, however, was not necessarily shared by the CLASH team, who (as mentioned above) simply found the management support on offer inadequate, irrespective of seniority or status:

"CLASH were three workers who have taken up an enormous amount of time, which they don't necessarily recognise or acknowledge. They felt unsupported, despite the fact that there's been an immense amount of support going on" (s).

The principle problem of management functioning, relevant to both intra-team and worker-manager relations, and rooted in the very structure itself, was summed up by one worker:

"There's an essential problem in that the reason that we haven't been managed terribly well is because there is no interface between us as a team and the management that do exist" (w).

This lack of 'interface' between the CLASH team and their Steering Group (which also existed between managers; see below) was aggravated by three related factors: the CLASH team's own difficulties in managing themselves effectively; the team's alliance with voluntary managers and their aim to mobilise voluntary participants into confrontation with statutory managers; and the Steering Group's own difficulties in managing itself in the context of an ongoing confrontation between voluntary and statutory sector managers (see below and also Chapter Five). It was this structural vacuum between the outreach team and its Steering Group of managers which allowed the CLASH team a disproportionate amount of autonomy and independence and gave the space for CLASH to manage themselves, at least on an everyday level, more or less as they wanted. It is ironic for the CLASH team to feel on the one hand "under-managed" while on the other wishing to manage themselves, and for the Health Authority to feel the workers "unsupported" despite the "immense amount of support" they clearly wished to give them. For this was essentially the problem. Without the skills to know how to work effectively within a Health Authority and to gain the management support they required, the CLASH team were unable to translate their expertise and knowledge about their clients and their service needs into constructive service development and delivery (see Chapter Five). The team had ideas about the direction of service changes on ground level but they experienced great difficulty in actually understanding, and certainly manipulating, the management process to their advantage.

This inability to negotiate effectively in the management of the project bore directly on the conflicts which also existed over the project's service delivery and plans for service development (see Chapter Seven). The views of two statutory managers provide further insight:

"As one of the principle objectives of the CLASH team is to access people into the Health Service, one would have thought you would specifically employ people who would have the skills in order to do that. What we did was to specifically employ people who had the skills to do outreach work - and that's what they've done successfully. We didn't employ people with the skills to manipulate and persuade the Health Service to change - and that's simply what they haven't done" (s).

"The administration in the Health Service by and large is highly unimaginative... with regard to service delivery. They are not interested in service delivery, they are interested in balancing the books, they're not really interested in 'quality of care', and don't understand the environment; neither do I. So, yes, I think they've had immense hostility and suspicion from quite senior levels, and lack the ability to understand in what world they're operating" (s).

So without the necessary go-between or interface between the CLASH team and management (apart from the team's 'alliance' with voluntary participants), there was little hope of the structure functioning in practice. This point is illustrated by looking briefly at a crucial but exceptional period during which worker-manager relations went well. While in post, one statutory manager in particular had established a good working relationship with the team, and had effectively facilitated interaction between the outreach team and the Health Authority. As one of the workers recounted:

"And he had no idea of - I mean, he just thought we were very weird creatures. But fairly quickly... I'd say after about six months, he really clicked onto us, and he really began to appreciate... what we were doing and how long it was taking... and... there was a definite switch in his attitude, and... he was basically completely and utterly on our side. He would circumvent normal Health Authority bureaucracy and procedures, just in simple things, like getting us detached work expenses, which the Health Authority had never heard of" (w).

This view meshed with the manager's:

"I think we were all fairly suspicious of them. They looked different, they behaved differently, they were rather arrogant in our eyes. A slight feeling of being God's gift - we weren't quite sure to what or for whom. But my involvement grew quite rapidly, because what seemed to be prejudicing the project in the very early days was people getting very defensive, people getting very aggressive; people just not understanding what the hell each other was about. As an administrator you have a little toe-hold in a very wide range of departments, professions, power groups and all that kind of thing. So I had enough of an insight into it all to see that if you could crack simple problems and if they didn't feel as if everybody was out to get them we could hold onto it a bit longer... So it gradually fell to me more and more to play the link role" (s).

This particular relationship between the CLASH team and statutory management was crucial in that it provided the interface which both outreach workers and managers had needed at precisely the point when it was needed. This interface was provided by a manager with a considerable, and perhaps an unusual, understanding of the requirements of outreach work and of the outreach team. He was acceptable to the outreach workers as well as being familiar with, and powerful enough, to deal with the administrative and bureaucratic structures of the Health Authority. Without him, the team's practical difficulties in confronting the complexities of Health Authority bureaucracy might have continued, and in the process could have hardened the divisions between outreach workers and statutory managers. His intervention, though clearly necessary in preventing the failure of collaborative links in the early days, was not sufficient to head off the eventual statutory-voluntary split which characterised much of CLASH's history. After this manager's departure, the management functioning once again became dominated by conflict. Once more the team would "stamp their feet", be seen as "petulant children" and the communication process (as viewed by CLASH) would consist of the team being "told to go away and write another paper" (w).

Voluntary-statutory relations: Ideology and power

We have suggested that the tensions operating between statutory and voluntary managers, and between statutory managers and outreach workers, stemmed from differences in the style and ideology of work and in conceptions of health and service provision as a whole. The voluntary sector, working closer to the principles of community-based and community-action models of health promotion, valued negotiation and participation with clients as one of the basic principles of outreach work. In contrast, there was a tendency for voluntary participants to view the Health Authority in top-down terms: as "desk-sitters", as a bureaucratic, inflexible and controlling organisation which favoured prescription to participation. These perceptions of the Health Service as inflexible and inaccessible, unable to understand the nature of outreach work or the needs of hard-to-reach populations, directly affected the response of voluntary managers to their statutory counterparts: "when CLASH started we realised what a horrible monster the Health Service is and what an incredible bureaucracy it is" (v).

Aware of this, one statutory manager explains:

"The view of the voluntary sector, which on the one hand was feeling that there should be more health input and HIV was becoming a real issue for their clients...[and]...that the Health Authority ought to do something, but if the Health Authority did something it was likely to be highly - it might be very, very, well, controlling and inflexible. So that tension was established from very early on and has existed throughout the project. On the one hand, there's the criticism of the Health Authority for not taking on the issues, but in fact when the Health Authority does take on the issues it's often seen as highly bureaucratic and very controlling, a tension around statutory organisations as agents of social control - not on the agenda quite as explicitly as that, but around" (s).

There was thus a fundamental "managerial cultural difference" between voluntary and statutory participants (s). As described by a statutory manager, the voluntary sector tended to manage by discussion and consensus, whereas the Health Service, since 1986 when general management was introduced, "were trying to get away from consensus management to leadership management, and the buck stops here decision making" (s).

These ideological differences, reinforced and reproduced by the tensions in worker-manager relations outlined above, were aggravated by what appeared to be a structural imbalance between voluntary and statutory representation in the collaborative organisation of the project. Voluntary participants on the Steering Group, for example, frequently felt that the balance of power and influence in the construction of policy and practice of the project was firmly weighted in favour of the Health Service, particularly given that the Management Group consisted entirely of statutory participants: "it [CLASH] was set up to have an imbalance in favour of the Health Service" (v). This tendency for decisions to be top-down was recognised as a problem by a member of the Management Group:

> "The fact that they would often come up with the initiatives for decisions and we would end up in the role of sanctioning or vetoing was one of the real tensions. They would say 'you're paying, but all initiatives, all suggestions, all the actual direction of the project is actually not coming from the Health Authority side', which was fair comment" (s).

Voluntary participants recognised the "tremendous kind of moral authority... that comes from the voluntary sector" where "if a group of voluntary sector workers get together and speak collectively on an issue, then it's very hard for the Health Authority to argue against it" (v), but nonetheless felt the ultimate veto and power, including over the budget, was in the hands of the Health Authority. As viewed by one of the CLASH workers and a voluntary manager:

> "Ultimately the power is always going to lay where the money is because we can suggest whatever we like and the voluntary groups can support us to the hilt but they're not paying" (w).

> "The Steering Group was going to be four of them (statutory) and four of us (voluntary). In fact it slipped through without agreement that it was to be chaired by someone from the Health Authority, not realising that that person had an incredible amount of power. As far as I was concerned their main job was to prevaricate and delay the decision making and to veto those decisions... " (v).

From the Health Service perspective, the Unit General Manager viewed the voluntary-statutory relationship in more co-operative terms, but the implications for power and control in practice were essentially the same:

> "They were at least equal partners on the Steering committee, the Steering Group decided on the Chair, the Health Authority did not just grab the high ground. We were paying for the team but we were also trying to learn from the voluntary sector about how this kind of activity would work. But I think there was an

acceptance from the voluntary sector, from day one almost, that we would be the senior partner by virtue of holding the budget and contracts of employment" (s).

Furthermore, since having endorsed the management consultant's proposals, the CLASH team has now been made accountable to the NHS hierarchy, and is to be directed on aspects of strategy and policy by an Advisory Group with no direct responsibility or power to make decisions. Although it is envisaged that the Advisory Group will consist of representatives from both sectors, there is no commitment to decisions being equally weighted or jointly made. In effect, rather than enhancing the possibilities for collaboration between voluntary and statutory styles of management, the 'voluntary' contribution will have been reduced to that of 'suggestion'. In the words of the quotes above, while the Health Authority hopes to continue to "learn from the voluntary sector about how this kind of activity should work", perhaps even expecting them to "come up with the initiatives for decisions", it is recognised that the Health Authority will endorse its power to "veto" and "sanction" whenever considered appropriate and necessary. This may indeed relieve the management process of one of its most central "tensions", but may be achieved at the expense of the project's original purpose. It was precisely these tensions which would have been expected from a collaboration of this nature, and precisely the purpose of the collaboration to resolve these through negotiation in the business of managing an integrated model of service provision. Exactly what the implications of this shift will be for the project's outreach work for the CLASH workers and for their clients is of course as yet unknown, although it is to some of these issues which we return in the chapters which follow.

Changing interests and levels of involvement

Changing levels of interest and involvement among the participants further compounded the problems of management functioning described above. Within the CLASH team, since the evaluation began there have been seven changes in full-time staff, three additional part time sessional workers appointed and one change in administrative staff. Since the evaluation was completed, there has been one further change in full-time staff, two changes in sessional staff and the appointment of one full-time locum worker. Such a high turnover of staff - although characteristic of projects of this nature - had direct implications on the team's internal management and decision making processes, while also inevitably affecting the tone and efficiency of worker-manager relations and service provision.

Staff changes and changing levels of involvement on the project's Steering and Management Groups had equally important implications for management functioning, often disrupting the flow of collaborative decision making. The attendance of participants on the Steering and Management Groups was increasingly variable and become a recurrent problem. Key figures in the statutory Management Group either found their attention and energy drawn elsewhere, left the Health Authority altogether, or were unable to attend meetings through pressure of work and other commitments. At times the day-to-day management of CLASH was limited to contact between outreach workers and individual Health Authority administrators, often by telephone. New functionaries appointed by the Health Service would be invited onto the Steering Group: "we were always having these statutory people wheeled in" (w). Different participants pursued their own agendas (relating to objectives, power, position, career) into which the existence or activities of CLASH were incorporated or co-opted. As described by one voluntary representative on the Steering Group:

"The Management Group of CLASH have to a certain extent individual vested interests, and by that I mean people that are nursing budgets and people who are nursing careers. At least one person on the Management Group made a definite bid to have the formation of CLASH as a step on their career ladder... even went so far as to say that it was their idea" (v).

Voluntary participation on the Steering Group was equally variable, and by early 1990, it was not unusual for voluntary representation to be non-existent. Levels of voluntary interest appear to have been influenced by two main factors. On the one hand, some voluntary participants felt they had achieved their objectives once the project was established:

"I think CLASH is established both internally and externally to the Health Authority. It's more on the map internally, therefore it experiences less difficulties in terms of the Health Authority internal management structure. Externally it's seen as being established and there's no immediate threat of it being cut or disbanded or whatever, so in some ways the external voluntary groups have been able to relax. With it up and running we can back off a little bit" (v).

On the other hand, with the balance of power in favour of the Health Authority, others felt that they were unable to achieve their objectives:

"It felt increasingly that we [voluntary] had very little actual power to do anything except to withdraw" (v).

"What gives influence is that you hold the purse strings, you can hire and fire. We [the voluntary sector] can do none of those things. We have no money, no accountability to the line management structure. We're separate to that. We have no influence except our ability to argue and stamp our feet or withdraw our support" (v).

Ironically, as some voluntary participants were aware, by their "non-attendance" they "were colluding" with the Health Authority's attempts to maintain power over the project. Attempts to encourage or to replace voluntary representatives on the Steering Group were slow to bring results. Finally, a diminishing level of voluntary sector interest, combined with the increasing statutory managerial control over the project - in part a function of there being little voluntary participation - meant that the explicit aims of collaboration became inoperable. While collaboration was pursued with some vigour in the initial stages of implementation - in a context of conflict, tension and potential disintegration - since the management consultant's proposed changes, the managerial atmosphere at the time of writing seems almost tranquil, with the project poised for change, ready to take on new hierarchical structures within the Health Authority.

CHAPTER FIVE

EVALUATING MANAGEMENT STRUCTURE AND FUNCTIONING

The problems encountered in management functioning were identified as primarily structural. These arose in part from oversights in management design, perhaps unwittingly encouraged by the urgency with which the project was established, the desire for the Health Authority to 'do something', and the firm intention of both voluntary and statutory sectors to collaborate. Collaboration was viewed as the most effective way to proceed, even if at the time the precise nature of how the collaboration was to function remained uncertain. Oversights in the design of the management structure were compounded in practice by a variety of factors, which brought to the idea of collaboration the terms in which it was to be experienced the many conflicts and tensions described above. At the various levels of the management process, the experiences of their problematic functioning provided rich insights as to the enormity and breadth of what it meant to collaborate. The integrated voluntary-statutory management of the CLASH outreach project was not simply a union between voluntary and statutory managers, but an attempted union of competing perspectives and ideologies about work, styles of management and conceptions of health, health education and service provision.

Attempting to untangle the problems of management in order to construct an interpretation on the precise sequence of events is complex. The management difficulties experienced may not have necessarily created insuperable problems in themselves. Rather they provide an accumulation of operational problems in project functioning, which in turn form useful foci for investigation, which we hope will generate practical guidelines for the future design and management of similar interventions. It would be a far less tangible task to attempt to elucidate precisely 'what caused what', isolating each element and its problematic and sequential functioning in practice. The general polarisation which occurred throughout the management process was a function of many factors. Arising more directly from the management structure itself were:

i   lack of definition and direction for internal team organisation and management;
ii   lack of management interface and accountability between the CLASH team and the Steering Group;
iii lack of clear lines of responsibility in power of organisation between voluntary and statutory participants on the Steering Group; and
iv   lack of clear lines of responsibility and accountability between the Steering Group and Management Group.

Feeding on these and at the same time contributing to their existence, and so reproducing their effects, were:

i   competing ideologies of management between the principles of collective working and NHS hierarchy;
ii   competing ideologies between styles of work and management between workers and statutory managers;
iii competing ideologies between styles of work and management between voluntary and statutory managers; and
iv   collusion between styles and management between workers and voluntary managers.

Each of these elements contributed towards making management functioning problematic at the three distinctive levels of management:

i   interface between the CLASH team and management;
ii   the Steering Group and the collaborative process;
iii everyday management and the Management Group.

Interface with management and collective functioning

We have suggested that many of the problems experienced in the functioning of the management structure stemmed from one simple oversight: the lack of an interface between the CLASH project and its management. Resulting from this were problems created by the initial management vacuum of non-direction which established a project without any guidelines for internal management and organisation, so permitting the team to build as a collective. This created its own problems of management as far as intra-team functioning was concerned but also reproduced and amplified other problems embedded in the management structure. These included the lines of responsibility and accountability between workers and managers (voluntary and statutory), as well as the lack of clarity in the lines of responsibility and organisation structured between voluntary and statutory managers on the Steering Group, and the nature of the collaboration itself. For example, how much was there a structural imbalance in the amount of power shared between voluntary and statutory managers and how much was this a shift by the Health Authority to gain control over a project proving itself unaccountable and difficult to manage?

There is no inherent reason for a collective not to operate both collectively and effectively. The CLASH team, however, rarely functioned as a collective. There were three reasons for this. First, the team operated as a "hidden hierarchy", where the more powerful workers dominated. This meant that the team's decision making process often resembled that of a hierarchy rather than that of a collective. Rather than becoming a source of strength within the team, the longer serving and more experienced workers became the source for tension and conflict, especially given the less experienced workers' desires for (at least) equality within the team. Second, and partly in response to the lack of trust generated between workers and the lack of belief in the team actually working as a collective, the team began to operate as a disparate collection of separate work identities, as rather more 'task-protected' than 'task-oriented', where individual workers fought for their protected corners of work interest and expertise. As a result, collective negotiation was actually discouraged by the team as they would actively exclude one other from constructive group discussions on the basis of area of work interest, gender, sexuality, life experience and so on. Third, and in the context of individual workers attempting to gain or retain power and control within the team, the team's weekly decision making meetings became a battlefield for these tensions. As a result, the possibilities for an efficient and succinct decision making process became suffocated by lengthy and complex discussion often involving personal battles between team members. With little trust and respect for fellow workers and with few clear lines of responsibility and accountability between them, decisions - when they were eventually made - were sometimes simply ignored when it came to action.

The functioning of CLASH's collective perhaps had little hope of working effectively largely because its foundations were too rigid and the commitment to democratic working too distant. The team's attempts to function completely 'equally' were perhaps short-sighted, and allowed individual workers little flexibility to make their own specific contributions to team work. Had the team been organised in a non-hierarchical but task-oriented fashion[1], individual workers may have had opportunities to realise their own areas of expertise as well as to provide direct feed back to the team. This would have allowed an element of reflexivity in team functioning. The team appeared to work in a fashion resembling 'task-orientation', but this had occurred on the basis of workers' attempts to gain some individual control or footing within the project. In practice, recent appointments to the project and less experienced workers had little chance of gaining a route into project work when recognition for particular work areas, once having been established, were carefully nursed and protected by longer standing, more experienced workers. That the team's collective appeared to lack a basis of democratic practice probably had less to do with the individual workers - who, at some level, appeared genuinely to believe in the principles of collective working - but may have related more to the structural context in which the collective emerged, the lack of direction and interface provided by the management structure, and the defensive responses this engendered in the team.

The team collective was in principle accountable to the Management Group for day to day administration and to the Steering Group for overall strategy and policy development. The CLASH team, however, had found itself - more by luck than judgement - able to make its own decisions both on day to day internal management procedures and on overall internal management strategy and policy. Not only had CLASH proved part of the management structure's functioning inoperable, they had actually established an ideological stratagem, and once the collective had been established many statutory managers became immobilised as to 'what to do next' and 'how to effectively manage the collective'. The Management Group, in particular, while able to manage the project more effectively on day to day Health Authority business (such as condom orders, contracts, appointment of new workers, project expenses and so on), proved unable to offer constructive suggestion as to the direction of the project's internal functioning. Beyond endorsing the team's recommendation for an external consultant to explore the efficiency of team dynamics and group processes, it seemed that managers could do little more than just watch from a distance, while the project workers, in effect, managed themselves as they pleased.

In this context, the CLASH team were keen to protect their autonomy and independence. Able to collude with voluntary participants - both on egalitarian methods of working and aspects of service delivery - and without an appropriate management interface between the team and its management groups, CLASH would arrive at Steering Group meetings able to control the flow of information about its activities, successes and failures. How was the Steering Group to direct the team's overall strategy and policy efficiently when it felt severely handicapped in its capacity to control the project and to know precisely what it was doing?

Indeed, the project became increasingly difficult to manage even on an everyday basis, where the team's refusal to understand NHS administrative bureaucracy meant the management of relatively simple procedures - such as making and receiving an order for condoms or the production of a leaflet - became the source for lengthy conflict between the CLASH team, voluntary participants and statutory managers.

The brief period in which an 'interface' was provided between the CLASH team and their managers makes clear the key requirement which was lacking in the management process: communication, in terms both the Health Authority and CLASH were ready and able to understand. Without this, neither the CLASH team nor the Health Authority could negotiate together effectively (voluntary managers provided much of the 'translation'). The problem in providing CLASH with the interface they required to 'work' the management process, therefore, was aggravated by the lack of control the Health Authority had over the project and the refusal of the workers to actually be managed. The question of how much the Health Authority actually wished to assist the CLASH team in becoming effective manipulators of the management process remains. Similarly, there remains a question as to how much CLASH were actually willing to learn, preferring instead to remain distanced from management, taking as they did (at least in appearance) a democratic egalitarian stance. The Health Authority's desire to exert control over the project (for example, by allowing the team to flounder at the point of negotiating a proposal for service changes) can be seen as similar to the team's own tactics of mobilising against the Health Authority in 'collectives' and 'alliances'. But as long as CLASH lacked these essential management skills - and the Management Group rarely provided the team with such supervision - the Health Authority were able to retain some control over the project, sanctioning, vetoing and playing for time as it saw fit, while the CLASH team became increasingly frustrated at their inability to "get what they wanted" so acting in the only way they knew - by "stamping their feet". This in effect meant attempts to restrict the team's efficacy in manipulating the management process were often simultaneously attempts to prevent the CLASH team pursuing particular service developments (see Chapter Seven).

A number of observations can be drawn from this summary. Principally, the management structure lacked a clear line of responsibility and accountability between the CLASH team and its management. Many of the difficulties which arose might have been avoided had the CLASH team been organised with clear internal management structures. The team's own decision making process and their subsequent lack of accountability to management might have been improved had decision making not occurred in isolation, and had the Management Group, or a representative from a similar body, been actively involved. The project might have been better able to operate collectively, in a non-hierarchical task-oriented manner, had there been clear lines of responsibility drawn between team members, the team's internal management process and the team's day to day managers. The Management Group in particular, failed in its function to provide the team with the supervision and direction it required to operate efficiently within the overall management process. Had the day to day internal organisation of the project worked more efficiently, the Steering Group may also have functioned more as planned, and much of the initial polarisation between outreach workers, voluntary participants and statutory managers been avoided.

Power, collaboration and the Steering Group

From the inception of the CLASH project there were discussions about whether the project should be located in the voluntary or statutory sector. As outlined earlier, the project was to remain as independent as possible while facilitating access for clients to statutory and voluntary health services. The channel through which the project was to be managed on a collaborative basis was the Steering Group. But almost as soon as the Steering Group began to meet, tensions arose between voluntary and statutory managers (amplified by the CLASH team's collusion with voluntary participants) over the style of management and direction of the project. The problem (as suggested earlier) was mutual - with both sides confronting each other in incomprehension. And this was in essence what was to be learned from such a collaboration: the expressions of 'difference' which emerged through the tensions and conflict, although seemingly destructive, provided insight into how each party operated and how different they were in their approaches to the organisation of service delivery and service development.

It was the collaboration between these differences in approach which the management structure of the CLASH project had hoped to build on in order to provide an integrated voluntary-statutory service provision to clients. As one voluntary manager commented:

"The voluntary groups in some ways act as a catalyst to stimulate the Health Authority to provide more direct provision relevant to the needs of street populations and the kind of stuff accessed through street work" (v).

In providing a management structure with a component for day to day managerial supervision and a component for overall collaborative direction on outreach strategy and policy, it was envisaged that the voluntary sector's experience and expertise in community work would be utilised to the best advantage:

"There are advantages in actually running that kind of parallel structure, because you have a direct line management which, if it is working efficiently, should be able to provide funds and resources and actual day to day practical management. On the other hand, having a Steering Group with a structure softens the line management and also continually acts as a sort of catalytic effect, stimulating it and keeping it on line in terms of what the actual needs might be in the fast moving outside world. I think these two things are in constant tension, but if they work together, it can make the actual management structure more relevant to what is going on" (v).

In practice of course, many voluntary managers found the Health Authority suffocating; so highly bureaucratic that they often felt unable to become a catalyst for appropriate service development in accordance with "what was going on". From the Health Authority's perspective much depended upon the statutory personnel involved. With the right people, the "creative thinkers" (s), gaps could be bridged, and the structure made flexible enough to function as planned, which is precisely what had occurred when CLASH were briefly provided with the interface they required to function with management. As a statutory manager explained:

"It [the Health Authority] does have the potential, but it only has the potential where there are creative thinkers within the Health Authority. The Health Authority is a bureaucracy and as such it tends to be quite conservative in its approach. But there are people within Health Authority's who like to think creatively about the work, and who actually get a positive buzz out of trying to make services more responsive and therefore meaningful for consumers. And whilst there are those people around, that potential is always there. It depends how influential they are and how much the organisation, in terms of it's own limitations, permits people to develop. But we are getting into a much more difficult scenario where the Health Authority is thrown back on itself... and being even more conservative because there has got to be funding for all this" (s).

Whether or not the Health Authority was responsive and flexible enough to cater for hard-to-reach clients' needs is discussed later, but here we can consider the problems encountered in the attempts to meet these aims through the collaborative management of the project on the Steering Group.

To summarise the findings presented in Chapter Four, the Steering Group found difficulty in achieving its collaborative aims largely as a consequence of the tensions which emerged between the CLASH team and statutory managers. This in turn resulted in a combative alliance being made between voluntary participants and outreach workers. With the CLASH team largely unmanageable, constructive and collaborative negotiation for the project's direction on outreach strategy and policy became submerged in the wider ongoing conflict between voluntary and statutory managers, with the CLASH team simply 'wanting to get its own way'. And this may have been central to the Steering Group's problematic functioning: as long as voluntary participants appeared to champion the CLASH team's recommendations for project management and service development, then in effect the Steering Group became a forum for negotiation between outreach workers once removed and statutory managers, rather than a space for clear headed negotiation between voluntary and statutory managers. This does not necessarily suggest that voluntary managers became drawn in by CLASH to their every wish and desire, but rather that the lines of responsibility and accountability between managers was just as blurred as that between the CLASH team and their Steering Group. It also demonstrates forcefully the cultural differences operating between the management styles of voluntary and community workers and the Health Service. For while it would be more usual practice in the Health Service for managers to negotiate between themselves and then impart recommendations and decisions from above (which may be one reason why the outreach workers themselves were 'in attendance' on the Steering Group), for voluntary representatives this process may often operate in the reverse. So while in principle the CLASH team were only observers on the Steering Group, voluntary participants nevertheless attempted to ensure that recommendations for service development involved the CLASH team as participants in the Steering Group's management process.

Even if the voluntary participants had been made more 'accountable' in Health Service management terms, the seeds of conflict between workers and managers had already been sown, and it is questionable whether voluntary or statutory participants would have responded any differently. Regardless of the extent of accountability between managers, there was a further compounding factor: the power relationship between voluntary and statutory managers was never fully articulated. Although most participants seemed to have worked on the assumption that the collaboration was 'equal', in terms of the number of participants represented from each sector and in terms of the process by which decisions were made, in practice the power in decision making was clearly weighted towards the Health Authority. This was probably unintended, but nonetheless had disruptive consequences for the practice of collaboration. Statutory managers, for example, found themselves in the role of sanctioning recommendations made by the Steering Group as a whole. This was largely as a result of BHA holding the budget for the project, and the corresponding constraints this brought to decision making. Perhaps the only way to have avoided this would have been to locate the financial administration of the project elsewhere, possibly between both sectors. Although not a practical suggestion at this stage, the most viable alternative might have been to establish the CLASH project as a relatively independent non-profit making company with a board consisting of both voluntary and statutory representatives, and with funding (or sponsorship) split between the Health Service and other charitable sources.

As a result of the feelings of increased powerlessness among voluntary participants, the regularity with which they attended meetings began to dwindle, many concluding that they were unable to make a truly collaborative contribution. The CLASH workers too, perceived this problem in similar terms: whatever the support which voluntary participants could give the project, it was often largely a matter of finance and bureaucratic procedure as to whether recommendations became endorsed.

With voluntary participation fast declining on the Steering Group, the possibilities for collaboration became ever more distant. At its worst, it was not uncommon for the Steering Group to consist exclusively of statutory participants, with the CLASH team as observers. This as we have suggested is not so much a fault of design as of circumstance. Without the conflicts emerging from within the team as a result of initial management oversights in the team's accountability to management, the management process might have functioned more collaboratively.

Many of the problems which emerged from the fact that power ultimately and unavoidably rested with the Health Authority and its budget, although being very much a part of design, may have been alleviated had clearer terms of accountability existed between voluntary and statutory managers and had the precise roles they were to play in the collaboration been fully articulated.

Everyday management and the problem of supervision

There were two basic lines of responsibility in day to day management outlined in the original terms of reference. First, that the team should be provided with day to day administrative direction and support, and second, with professional management and supervision.

Day to day administrative management at least functioned regularly. The continuity of this provision, however, was disrupted by staff changes and the changing levels of interest of the managers concerned. Like the management process as a whole, lines of responsibility and accountability between the CLASH team and managers became increasingly blurred. Although the day to day administration of the project was to be concerned with everyday Health Authority procedures, in the context of the team's frustrations with statutory managers and their concerns to protect their own position of autonomy within the management structure, the facilitation of the project's administration became a painful process. Once more, the team seemed unable to understand the necessity of NHS bureaucracy, and the administration of relatively straight forward procedures became the focus of ongoing battles between workers and managers.

The source of this problem - endemic to the functioning of the management process as a whole - was rooted in the divergence of management styles between voluntary and statutory sectors. The CLASH workers were familiar with a style of management in which once decisions were made, action became immediately possible, while the Health Authority demanded that its workers complete a variety of paper work, be accountable for what they do and spend, and wait an undefined length of time for an outcome. The incapacity of the bureaucracy to do anything quickly added to the workers' increasing alienation from the Health Authority. The examples cited in Chapter Four (purchasing of office equipment and employment of staff) demonstrated the team's lack of expertise in dealing with NHS styles of management and administration, their unwillingness to learn, and their desire to compete against them.

Many of the difficulties in the administrative management of the project may have been alleviated had the CLASH team included a worker with experience of NHS management. This would have provided a more realistic platform on which to base project recommendations, making them less alienated from the realities of NHS management, and avoiding at least some of the polarisation in communication between outreach workers and the Management Group. In turn, this may have also improved intra-team functioning, as lines of accountability between the CLASH team and managers might have become clearer for workers. Similarly, as we suggested above, the problems of polarisation at the point of communication between workers and managers might also have been alleviated had a representative from the Management Group (or similar) taken more of an active role in the decision making processes and internal management of the team.

The problems encountered in the professional management and supervision of the CLASH team also stemmed from the differences between management styles. While professional supervision is usual practice within the Health Service, the CLASH workers presented specific problems to the clinical psychologist concerned in terms of the unusual nature of their work. Ideally, the outreach workers required supervision from managers with both direct experience of NHS management and an understanding of detached outreach work. Despite attempts to provide the CLASH workers with supervisors to their individual requirements, appropriate personnel could not be found, at least within the Health Authority. Eventually, compromises were made and supervisors were found. The clinical psychologist on CLASH's Management Group began to provide the male workers with supervision himself, while one of the female workers arranged supervision externally.

The problem of being unable to find appropriate supervisors for the CLASH team within the Health Authority was perhaps unavoidable. With little experience of outreach work, of the communities to which the intervention was addressed, or indeed of community workers themselves, it really is no surprise. Although professional supervision is conventionally part of the Health Authority's system of 'in-house' management, it probably would have been only possible to provide the CLASH workers with the supervision they required from the voluntary sector. In this case, the problem of supervision arose from the management structure itself, which had designated the Health Authority with the responsibility to do the everyday managing, and voluntary managers with the shared responsibility of directing on policy and practice. There was never really a possibility of collaboration between voluntary and statutory managers concerning the CLASH project's everyday management, precisely because the project was statutory, no matter how the workers saw their own or their project's identity. In this respect, a learning process has occurred - partly as a result of the experience of collaboration - where the workers' professional supervision needs are currently being met within the Health Authority.

New management structures: Poised for change

The management consultant invited by the Steering Group made a number of recommendations for a revised management structure, which is represented in the figure below (Figure 5.1).

Figure 5.1   Proposed revised management structure
(expanded from Dorn, 1990)

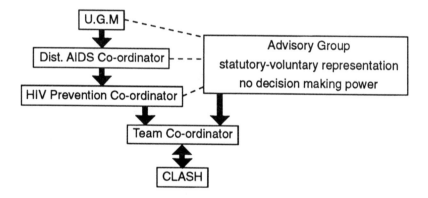

The principle changes to the project's existing management structure (see Figure 4.1, page 51) involved the creation of a managerial co-ordinating position within the CLASH team and the replacement of the Steering and Management Groups with an Advisory Group. The recommendations put forward by the management consultant were three-fold (Dorn, 1990):

First, that a project co-ordinator should be appointed within the team in April 1991, or as soon as practical thereafter. The job specification should cover the direction of the project's outreach work, including practice, supervision of all staff, including oversight of induction and staff training, liaison with departments within the Health Authority, relevant outside organisations and the media, lines of accountability to line management, lines of accountability to an advisory committee, and quarterly non-managerial supervision.

Second, the co-ordinator should be the supervisor and line manager for all full time and part time workers and the administrator. The UGM would be line manager to the co-ordinator, although it was later decided that the co-ordinator will be immediately accountable to the District HIV Prevention Co-ordinator, in turn accountable to the District AIDS Co-ordinator, in turn accountable to the UGM. Additionally, non-management supervision should be offered to the co-ordinator on a quarterly basis, and to prevent confusion of roles, no further supervision should be provided by members of the Advisory Group.

Third, the existing Steering and Management Groups should be replaced by an Advisory Group consisting of current members (or equivalents) of the Steering and Management Groups. The Advisory Group will have no responsibility to 'steer' or 'manage' the project. The group's main responsibility will be to meet once a year to approve the CLASH project's Annual Report, an internal Report to the Health Authority, and the coming year's work plan. It will also meet on three other quarterly occasions to review progress and, additionally, at the request of the project co-ordinator. The co-ordinator and one other CLASH worker (rotating) would be full members of the Advisory Group.

The consultant's recommendations for a team co-ordinator were clearly an attempt to provide the point of interface required between the CLASH team and their managers. The type of person appointed will be crucial to the communication process and the subsequent smooth running of the project. In this respect the consultant recommended that the co-ordinator would have both a good working knowledge of NHS management and of outreach and community-oriented intervention. Given their previous experiences of attempting to find such "creative thinkers" with management skills, some statutory managers of the Steering Group thought this would be almost impossible, and saw the potential for the co-ordinator to "be set up to fail" (Fieldnotes of Steering Group meeting, 1990). From the perspective of the team's efficacy of internal functioning and its corresponding relation to managers, the co-ordinator's post will be a very precarious one to occupy. In the context of the team's desires for hierarchy having arisen as a result of the dysfunction between the principles and practices of collective working rather than through a genuine belief in such styles of management, and given the collusion of working styles with those of voluntary rather than statutory managers, it may be difficult for the co-ordinator to provide the interface required. Put simply, so much will depend upon whether the team *like* working with the co-ordinator, and this will depend as much on his or her ability to 'think creatively' and to demonstrate sufficiently the knowledge and skills relevant to the work, as it will on his or her perceived identity as a worker - as 'voluntary', 'community', 'statutory' and so on. If the team were to perceive the co-ordinator as possessing the qualities of a 'manager' (in 'statutory' terms), without an affinity for the needs of outreach work, rather than those of 'facilitator' or 'team leader', the interface may run the risk of being severely disrupted. All this may be further compounded by the fact that the team have little confidence in the Health Authority selecting a candidate with direct experience of detached outreach work.

The co-ordinator, however, at least has the weight of statutory line management to his or her advantage. Despite this, the potential for problems may be heightened by the consultant's recommendation to replace the existing Steering Group with a group of advisors with little or no decision making power. This is not to suggest that existing structures should have remained in place, but rather to make explicit the fact that because these changes involve the re-organising of CLASH closer to statutory management hierarchy they bring to the team exactly those styles of management and organisation which they have so fervently opposed. In effect, the Advisory Group restricts the potential of 'voluntary' input to that of 'suggestion', minimising what little power voluntary managers had to contribute to decision making on the Steering Group. This may mean that it has now been *officially* recognised that the Health Authority will sanction and veto recommendations as and when necessary. This clearly goes against the original aims of the collaboration to provide an integrated approach to service provision and decision making. It may also leave the CLASH team rather isolated, without the voluntary support they so much relied upon to further their suggestions for service development. In this context, there probably will be less scope for the CLASH team to participate efficiently in the management process and possibly less opportunity for the encouragement of 'bottom-up' and community based service development.

With the decision making process weighted in favour of the Health Service, and with little participation encouraged from the CLASH workers themselves, the effectiveness of the new management structure will largely depend on the 'creative thinking' qualities of the co-ordinator and his or her abilities to 'work' the management process to CLASH's advantage. This is why it is so important that the co-ordinator appointed has direct experience of community based health work as well as of NHS management. If this is not the case, there may be the possibility that the decisions made by the Advisory Group will have little basis in the experiences of doing outreach work (which are critical to making appropriate decisions on service delivery, service developments etc.), even if they are based on sound statutory management skills. Given that it is probably unlikely that such an 'ideal' co-ordinator will be appointed (when this interface was provided previously, it was very short-lived and provided by a manager with 'unusual' qualities), it may have been more beneficial to think in terms of a management structure which would aim to empower the outreach workers themselves (or at least voluntary managers) to communicate effectively with managers and to make appropriate suggestions and recommendations for service developments. Appointing a co-ordinator in the hope that this will provide the much needed interface between workers and managers may be only one option. It may also be viewed as an attempt by the Health Authority to solve the problem of management without confronting the problems which the CLASH team experienced in translating their ideas for community based service developments into appropriate action and service provision. Put another way, it is questionable whether this new structure will be as committed to the development of innovative and community based services as it will be to efficiently managing the CLASH team. This may be because the Health Authority found the style and nature of services encouraged by outreach workers and voluntary managers to be inappropriate for the Health Authority to encourage and provide, perhaps because they were perceived as essentially non-statutory services (see Chapters Seven and Eight). As a result, the new management structure, with its tendency for top-down decision making and corresponding lack of opportunity for outreach workers to participate fully, may actually alienate the CLASH team further, and contribute to precisely the sort of discontent which it intends to alleviate.

The new management structure therefore gives the Health Authority a greater position of control: the CLASH team are to be directly accountable to a series of line managers. Without the same level of commitment to collaboration and joint management, CLASH has now almost become a fully fledged statutory project (all the Health Authority needs to do now is suggest the disbanding of the Advisory Group). This may have profound effects for the nature of the service. First, it may involve for the workers a perceived deprofessionalisation of outreach as 'community work'. Having lost the voluntary support on which they were so dependent in their "fight against the statutory", their identity as community workers may have been compromised. With no apparent proof that they are working in a voluntary managed project, there may be little belief in the capacity of their new management structure to develop services in direct response to the needs of clients or 'the community'. This brings us to the second point. The ability for services to be flexible and responsive according to client need is fundamental to the principles of outreach and community work. If CLASH are unable to fully participate in the management process, and if this is also the case for the new-found voluntary 'advisors', there may be a real possibility of the outreach service becoming institutionalised within the Authority. Rather than empowering the workers to 'work' the management process themselves and building into the management structure mechanisms to ensure that service developments are planned according to clients' needs as opposed to managers' perception of those needs, the effectiveness with which required service developments can be negotiated will depend largely on the ability (and commitment) of the co-ordinator to effect change within the Health Authority. For the co-ordinator to achieve this, not only will he/she have to possess the unusual 'creative thinking' qualities demanded by such a position, he/she will require a position of power and influence within the Health Authority not made available to such a post. Along with the loss of autonomy and independence which may occur as a result of the management's re-structuring, lie the concomitant fears of service delivery being managed from above (and from above the co-ordinator) in an authoritarian and prescriptive manner.

So, are the consultant's recommendations for a new management structure an improvement on the existing structure by which the CLASH project had been managed for the last four years? Clearly, something had to be done. There is little point in attempting collaboration if managers and workers were unable to collaborate. The root of subsequent management problems was at the level of internal team functioning. In providing a team co-ordinator who will also act as a line manager between the team and the Health Authority, the team's internal management problems may indeed be resolved, if not at least controlled. The team co-ordinator also satisfactorily replaces the Management Group's responsibilities for the team's day to day management and administration.

Our findings, however, suggest that it might also have been practical to have made the CLASH team's line manager/team leader responsible to an integrated Steering Group which, as it originally existed, had the overall responsibility for direction on strategy and policy. A structure of this kind would involve CLASH's team leader receiving supervision and management from within the Health Authority (as in the new management structure), but would require re-negotiating and clearly defining the lines of responsibility and accountability between members of the Steering Group. This would be necessary in order to ensure that all participants were aware of the potential extent of their involvement as well as fully committed to providing this on a regular and continued basis. In particular, there would be a need to make the terms of the collaboration explicit in relation to decision making, especially regarding the levels of power, involvement and commitment from voluntary participants. The team leader would require both experience of NHS management and of community work, and would have room to organise internal management structures within the team according to mutual agreement between him/ herself, the team and the Steering Group. It would be the responsibility of the team leader to negotiate with outreach workers to ensure that clients' needs are reflected in the team's work and in their recommendations for future service developments. Although the team leader would have ultimate responsibility for the internal management of the CLASH team and for co-ordinating team decisions concerning appropriate recommendations for service delivery, it would be the mutual responsibility of the team leader as well as of the outreach workers to negotiate these recommendations through Steering Group. It is essential that the outreach workers themselves would have an active and participative role in this process as they are most aware of clients' needs and the feasibility of service options. It is equally important that voluntary managers experienced in community work would be fully involved in the decision making in order to advise the outreach team and statutory managers as to the appropriateness of these recommendations at the level of management. This structure (Figure 5.3) is in principle an intermediate version of the existing and newly proposed structures, but would encourage:

i.   the possibility for non-hierarchical task oriented management within the team if so desired (which would be overseen and managed by the team leader);

ii. accountability within the team concerning internal team management;

ii. a direct interface and accountability between the team and Steering Group;

iii. immediate accountability and direction between the team and Health Authority through the team leader on issues of day to day management and administration;

iv. the direction of project work to be organised through collaboration, with a commitment to pursuing service developments as required, so preserving the aims of the project to 'bridge gaps' by integrating responses to service provision.

In preserving links with the community through direct participation of the outreach workers and other community project managers in the management process, this structure would retain the aims of outreach to provide flexible services which reflect clients' expressed needs, and would encourage real innovation in practice.

Figure 5.2 Alternative recommended management structure

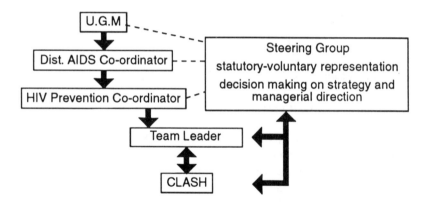

Having offered an alternative management structure, we should note that many other revisions and changes to CLASH's existing management structure could be recommended. Much depends upon what the management process aims to achieve. Our findings, which demonstrate the existence of tension and conflict between workers and voluntary and statutory managers, also show these responses to be both valid and useful. The tensions existing between voluntary and statutory managers on aspects of management, work styles, service delivery and ideological positioning, were precisely the differences in approach which the collaboration aimed to 'bridge' to mutual good effect in order to meet the needs of the hard-to-reach. Although the collaboration was almost suffocated by conflict, this is definitely not to say that nothing was learned and nothing was gained. The collaboration did produce conflict, but it also produced results. The point here is that had the management consultant been briefed by the Steering Group to the effect that the management structure was to remain explicitly collaborative retaining the possibilities for voluntary-statutory joint management, his recommendations might have looked slightly different. On the basis of our findings, we feel that the management structure, although desperately in need of revision, might have allowed the collaboration another chance to breathe. Of course, the proposed changes to the management structure do involve an element of collaboration, but the problem is that the terms of the collaboration are weighted potentially so as to lose that which made the project such an innovative creation.

Despite our attempts to imagine the potential problems of the new management structure, it is salutary to note that in practice there are probably no 'perfect' forms of organisation or management structure. Rather:

"structures are tools which can be created, selected and used by groups to attempt to achieve co-ordination and control in relation to their objectives. They will, like all tools, incur costs as well as benefits. The art of organisation design thus becomes one of selecting the most appropriate tool" (Dawson, 1986).

In this sense, chosen structures will inevitably be affected by the environments in which they operate. They will be affected by the objectives and strategies of interest groups involved, by people, their interests, motivation and performance, and by the processes of change and development within the organisation. The evaluation findings presented are a testament to this. Having identified and discussed some of the problems in CLASH's management process and functioning, we hope that we may have facilitated the design of the most appropriate 'tools' for the implementation of future similar management structures.

CHAPTER SIX

OUTREACH CONTACT AND SERVICE DELIVERY

Here we present qualitative and quantitative evaluation findings on the work of CLASH, concentrating on the project's detached outreach work. The chapter first outlines the scope and balance of the team's outreach and training work and summarises the extent of outreach contact and re-contact with clients. This is followed by findings on CLASH's detached outreach contact and service delivery which is reported in three sections: making detached contact; new clients; and re-contacted clients.

Note on the scope and balance of outreach work

The CLASH project's outreach work was divided between detached and peripatetic outreach work. The team's peripatetic outreach and training work covered sessions undertaken with staff and clients at a range of organisations working with young people, the homeless, drug users, prisoners and people with HIV infection and AIDS: Hungerford Drug Project, BHA's syringe exchange, Holloway Prison, Middlesex Lodge, Rufford Street Hostel, Bina Gardens Hostel, Haberdashers Hostel and City Roads[1]. We are unable to comment on the content and effectiveness of the team's peripatetic and training work in detail, as neither of these activities were formally monitored. Nevertheless, as we described in Chapter Three, CLASH successfully negotiated regular access into a variety of organisations and institutions. In particular, sessions have been undertaken regularly at Holloway Prison and at Middlesex Lodge since 1989. Both of these sessions were effective in reaching women usually out of contact with health services, and afforded occasional opportunities for more depth one-to-one counselling. The team's peripatetic work with drug users at syringe exchanges was undertaken largely in order to gain initial contacts and outreach work experience. We feel that it was appropriate that once the CLASH project was established it later focused it's peripatetic work away from syringe exchanges and towards organisations where clients had less access to HIV related health services. CLASH allocated a far greater proportion of project time to undertaking detached outreach work (see below), and we feel the proportion of time committed to peripatetic work and the institutions where this work was undertaken appropriately reflected client need and the team's objectives to provide services and referral access for clients considered hard-to-reach. The project's detached outreach work is discussed in more depth below.

Although the precise balance between detached and peripatetic work in terms of time and resources invested by the project varied over time, we illustrate below - albeit very crudely - the typical weekly commitments allocated by the team to detached and peripatetic work (Figure 6.1). In general, the CLASH team allocated proportionately more project time to peripatetic work than to detached work in the initial years (before mid 1988) and proportionately more project time to detached than to peripatetic work in more recent years (post 1989), than is represented in the figure.

Figure 6.1   Typical weekly time allocation and commitments 1989/90

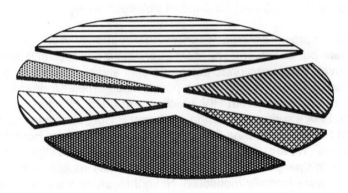

		hours per week	percentage
▨	Administration/other	20	14
◺	Drop in	13	9
▨	Management	43	31
≡	Detached	49	35
▨	Meetings	9	7
▨	Peripatetic	6	4
	Total	140	

Over a typical week (or weekly equivalent), the team had a total of 140 hours of project time (35 hours a week, with an average of four full-time workers and discounting sessional staff). The team allocated approximately 35% (49 hours) of their total weekly time to detached outreach work, and 4% (six hours) to peripatetic outreach work. Since 1989, the team also devoted a further 9% of project time (approximately thirteen hours) to clients with the introduction of the Friday drop-in service. In principle, this meant approximately half of the project's time (48%; 68 hours) was allocated to work directly with clients.

Although we must accept these as quite crude indicators of the project's activities in practice (which we summarise below), it is striking that only 35% of total project time was devoted to detached outreach work, and only half of total project time to client based work. This balance - both between detached outreach work and other client based work, and between client based work and other activities, had direct implications for the course of project work and on the extent to which the project was able to achieve its stated objectives concerning detached outreach work (see also Chapter Seven). The remaining half (52%; 72 hours) of weekly project time was split between visitors' meetings and attending outreach and practice related meetings (7%; 9 hours), and attending management and supervision related meetings (31%; 43 hours), with a total of 20 hours (14%) of total project time remaining for administrative and other client business.

Of most significance here, is the large amount of weekly equivalent time allocated to management meetings. Split between the team's internal management review meeting (17%; 24 hours), internal team management consultancy (9%; 12 hours), workers' supervision (3%; 4 hours) and attendance at Steering Group and Management Meetings (2%; 3 hours), the team allocated almost as much weekly time to management as they did to undertaking detached outreach work.

In practice, the Random Weekly Timetables (completed by workers on average once every four weeks over two six month periods) show that the team often spent less time than would have been allocated in a typical week actually doing detached and peripatetic outreach work, and proportionately more time attending meetings, staff training and undertaking administration work. The completed timetables show that of the total project hours available, only 27% were spent undertaking client based work: 16% on detached outreach work and 11% doing peripatetic outreach, training, client drop-in and client appointments. In striking contrast, more time was spent in management related meetings than any other single activity (25%): 18% doing project administration, and a further 16% in other meetings and staff training. The remaining 14% of project time, was spent with workers on holiday (12%) and off sick (3%).

Once again it must be stressed that these figures must be treated with caution. Nearly a third of the RWTs completed were felt to be 'untypical' by the outreach workers completing them. Throughout one of the periods one of the male workers had withdrawn from detached outreach work with the result that many outreach sessions with rent boys were cancelled (see below). Throughout another of the periods one worker was receiving induction and training. But there is no question that not only could the project have planned to allocate proportionately more time to detached outreach work and less to management and administration, in practice - when it actually came to doing the work - the team also appeared to mismanage and misdirect the investment of their time. This resulted in less time being devoted to the most fundamental of project goals: detached outreach work.

Note on the reliability of monitoring data

As previously outlined in Chapter Two, the nature of outreach work presented a number of specific problems for the systematic monitoring and evaluation of project outcomes and process performance measures. In general, we are confident that the majority of outreach contacts have been recorded by the team and aware that a small minority have gone unrecorded (largely contacts with street working women prostitutes). We are also aware that there is an increased likelihood of uncertainty about client information in our sample than would be the case had the target population been less transient and more open to lengthy contact and re-contact. This is a problem which is inevitable in evaluations of this type, and the feasibility and reliability of evaluation methodologies are likely to be more restricted when applied to outreach and community oriented intervention than when applied to agency based service responses. It is for this reason that inferences and generalisations drawn from the quantitative data presented here, particularly in relation to client HIV transmission and health behaviour, are made with caution.

Summary of outreach contacts, 1988-1990

Monitoring of the team's outreach contact with clients for the purposes of this evaluation began in January 1988 and ended in July 1990. The monitoring included contacts made with clients in detached outreach settings and at the project's office, and did not include contact with clients in group, training or peripatetic outreach settings. The CLASH team continue to monitor their services internally - including both detached and peripatetic work - for the purposes of informing appropriate service development and provision.[2]

Throughout the 31 month monitoring period, the team (since April 1989 consisting of four full-time and one part-time worker) made contact with 741 new clients (Figure 6.2). The number of contacts with new clients in any one evening ranged from none to twenty-four. Approximately half of new contacts were women (46%) and half men (54%). The mean age of new clients was 23 years (SD=7.0), with a range of 14 to 55 years. The majority (83%) of clients were described by the team as 'White British', with 7% described as 'Black British', 4% as 'White European', 2% as 'Irish', and 4% of unknown ethnicity.

Figure 6.2   Total number of client contacts: 1988-1990

Year	new contacts	re-contacts	total contacts
1988	348	124	472
1989	213	238	451
1990*	180	280	460
Total	741	642	1383

*   includes the first seven months of 1990

Further outreach re-contacts were made with 188 (25%) of these clients, a total of 642 times, giving an overall total of 1383 separate outreach contacts with 741 different clients (Figure 6.2). Thus three-quarters (75%; 533) of clients were contacted once (new clients), while the remainder were re-contacted an average of three times each (range 1-25), as Figure 6.3 below shows.

Figure 6.3   Distribution of outreach re-contacts 1988-1990

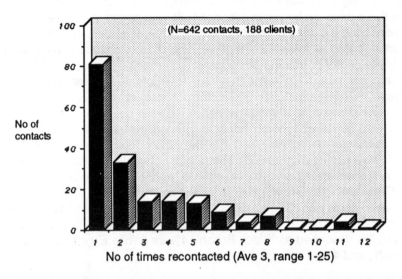

No of times recontacted (Ave 3, range 1-25)

The total number of outreach contacts remained relatively stable over the first two years (1988 and 1989), although the number of new client contacts and client re-contacts were variable from month to month within years. Thus, the average monthly total outreach contacts in 1988 was 39, in 1989 was 38, and in the first seven months of 1990 increased to 66. During this time, the average monthly contacts with new clients dropped from 29 in 1988 to 18 in 1989 (a drop of 39%) before rising to 26 in 1990, near to that of 1988. The average monthly re-contacts increased from 10 in 1988 to 20 in 1989 to 40 in 1990. Figures 6.4 and 6.5 below show this variability in terms of four monthly periods since 1988, and monthly averages over the three years.

Figure 6.4 Total outreach contacts 1988-1990

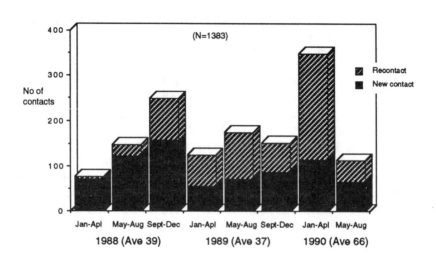

Figure 6.5 Monthly (mean) average new and re-contacts

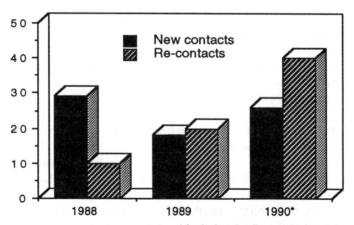

* includes the first seven months of 1990

Beyond the wider evaluation issues involved in interpreting the team's level of outreach contact as a function of time and resources invested, and style and nature of working practices (discussed in Chapter Seven), we can briefly consider here the reasons for the fall in the number of new clients contacted in 1989 compared with the previous and following years.

As a recent survey of HIV outreach intervention in the UK suggested, one of the central factors influencing the rate of outreach contacts with new clients is staffing (Hartnoll *et al.*, 1990; Rhodes *et al.*, 1991b). In short, the greater the resources in time and staffing devoted to outreach work, the greater the corresponding number of outreach contacts. In the case of CLASH, changes in the level of staffing can be seen to have brought about the decline in new client contact rates, particularly with male clients, in the first three quarters of 1989.

Throughout 1989, levels of staffing and staff input within the team varied. During the previous year the team had consisted of three full-time workers, all of whom undertook detached work in collaboration with other projects: one male worker in collaboration with the Soho Project working one detached session with rent boys a week; and two female workers, sometimes in collaboration with a worker from the Hungerford Project, working two detached sessions a week with women prostitutes. In January 1989 a male worker, in March a female worker, and in April a female sessional worker were also appointed. Throughout the first half of 1989, therefore, each of the new workers were involved in staff induction and training with existing full-time workers for periods of up to three months.

The most significant factor in the reduction of contacts, however, was the withdrawal of one of the two full-time male workers from detached outreach work (see also Chapter Four for management implications). One worker commented that only "one or two sessions - and I think I'm being generous in saying two" were undertaken before he withdrew from detached work completely. As another worker explained:

> "What was said was that he came here burnt out. But what I feel is that it was quite threatening. That he'd done a very different kind of street work... The other thing I think is that he was very interested in lots of other things that were going on in his life, and he was very involved in other projects that perhaps had more of a social life attached to them than this... I'm just telling you what we heard but the actual reason could have been all or any of them" (w).

As the project operated a policy of always working in pairs to ensure workers' and clients' safety, and matched workers' characteristics as much as possible to those of clients on aspects of gender and sexuality to facilitate the work, this meant that the regularity of detached work sessions with rent boys fell dramatically throughout mid 1989. Whereas outreach contact with women prostitutes, once having been established, steadily increased through to 1989, new contacts with rent boys were in fast decline (Figure 6.6). This in turn resulted in a decline in the total number of new contacts compared with previous and following years.

Figure 6.6 Contacts with rent boys and women prostitutes 1988-1990

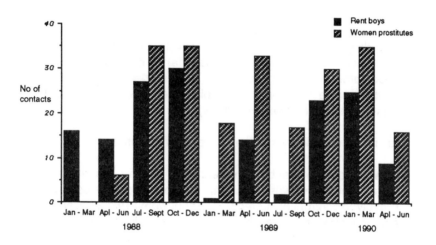

Reaching out: Making detached contacts

The majority (76%) of contacts with new clients were 'cold' contacts, as opposed to having been made by other methods, such as by 'snowballing' (10%), by clients initiating the contact (8%), or by other projects (most commonly the Hungerford Drug Project, the Soho Project and Streetwise Youth[3]) initiating the contact (6%).

The vast majority (97%) of contacts with new clients were 'face to face' contacts, with only 3% being client initiated 'phone calls. Of the face to face contacts, 85% were made via detached work, either on the streets (41%), in pubs (23%), at women prostitutes' flats (13%), in cafes (4%) or at other locations (4%). The remaining face to face contacts (15%) were made at the CLASH office, and throughout 1988, at the Hungerford Drug Project and at Bloomsbury's Cleveland Street syringe exchange (known as 'The Exchange'), where CLASH had worked initially to establish a foundation for drug related outreach and collaborative work. Of the total street based contacts (41%), most (66%) were located in King's Cross (in areas surrounding the station), 23% were based in Piccadilly, and the remaining 11% in Soho, Victoria and other locations. All contacts in pubs and at women prostitutes' flats were based in Soho.

Developing the detached work was a lengthy process. The three original CLASH workers had little experience of detached outreach work, and although one of the workers:

> "understood the nature of detached work... she'd never worked with drug users or prostitutes exclusively, or rent boys, and I mean I don't think in the early stages that we did have any - any notion of what it was about. I mean, I first started to get a feel for it when, quite early on, we did placements with... the Soho, Basement and the Hungerford" (w).

This view is echoed by another of the original workers:

> "It would appear that both the team and workers at that stage were frightened of working with those types of groups because it involved confronting stereotypes about women working, about pimping, about punters, about how you actually do the work. It was new work and they'd [the other two workers] got no idea about how to do it and had no direct experience of the scene themselves" (w).

Initial experience of detached outreach work was gained therefore from collaborative work with voluntary agencies undertaking similar work in central London. This is borne out by the increased number of new client contacts made through or at other agencies in the early months of 1988 as compared to latter parts of the year and in 1989.

But beyond the experience gained while workers were on placement, the CLASH team felt the project had been expected to undertake its detached work having been established "with no structures" (w). In this respect, the establishment of detached work was a trial and error process, particularly with work with women prostitutes, where there were no projects conducting similar work with which to collaborate or from whom to seek advice. One worker commented on setting up detached work in Soho with women prostitutes working from flats:

"I remember it being quite a frightening experience. We didn't know how we were going to be received, we didn't know what the set up was with these women, whether they had pimps. What we did at first was we just went round with a whole load of materials, you know, like 'we're from CLASH, here's our leaflet, here's how we can help you, here's some condoms'; and I mean the condom thing was the real kind of way of getting in... I mean we just went on the rampage basically around Soho, and we knocked on every single door that had a red light or had a poster up, and got rebuffed by probably fifty per cent of the people that we approached" (w).

The need for regular outreach sessions over long periods of time in order to establish a new area of work became apparent when undertaking participant observations in Euston. Euston station area was previously untouched by detached work. Fieldwork notes from observations show that the first three street work sessions (each lasting approximately six hours) were taken up with surveillance and observation:

"Again we spent most of our time just observing the movements in the station from a good viewing point. Much of what I was doing as an 'outreach worker' was similar to doing observational research. We were just clocking people's movements, watching people's contact, looking for connections between them..." (Fieldnotes, 1990).

The observations conducted at Euston showed evidence of a scene, albeit a small and subtle one. As a result, a decision was made to continue with regular street work sessions on the concourse. Fieldwork notes from subsequent sessions show the levels of ambiguity involved in actually attempting to cold contact rent boys at Euston:

"Having watched this boy for sometime propped against [name of shop], [name of co-worker] said to try and make a contact. This was our first attempt to cold contact at Euston. We moved over slowly towards him, me following [name of co-worker] some distance behind - he [the boy] saw us, looked a little nervous, and at this point [name of co-worker] said to 'pass', and we walked on by... " (Fieldnotes, 1990).

The problems of making initial cold contacts were heightened since outreach workers were not too sure that there was a scene at Euston. There was a problem of determining exactly the nature of the scene - was it boys cruising and cottaging[4] or a rent scene? Without a clear understanding of the nature of the scene itself, actively contacting boys was problematic - there was little or no assurance that these contacts were rent boys.

Without such assurances over time, and given the opacity of the scene - which on subsequent observations appeared more likely to be a cottage than a rent scene - after a total of five sessions, street work was abandoned. In contrast, in the case of King's Cross, where the prostitution scene was more evident, making initial cold contacts was more dependent on workers' having the 'courage of their convictions' than working through ambiguities and subtleties:

> "It was just a question of combing the streets and combing the bars, and just going up and taking your courage in your hands, and approaching a woman and saying very, very, very quickly, this is what we're doing, this is where we're from" (w).

Early surveillance and observation work in Victoria (December 1989) had also showed the rent scene to be far more visible than that possibly operating in Euston:

> "It certainly is a very busy rent boy area, with [name of shop] the clear focal point; boys waiting on one of the four corners - waiting for punters to approach" (Workers' Day and Night Book, 1989).

Subsequent observations by the team showed there to be optimum times of the day for targeting detached sessions; "two shifts of rent boys - the rush hour shift and the late shift" (Workers' Day and Night Book, 1990).

To establish new areas of detached work, therefore, demands lengthy periods of patient and systematic observation and surveillance - or "foot slogging" (v). It is only on this basis that contacting strategies can be planned, approaches prepared, and appropriate areas of service provision developed. But once this planning has been completed, there remain many and varied potential obstacles to complicate the process of contact with new clients. Of most concern for workers was the extent of police activity and safety.

Clients became more mobile and less open to contact when areas were policed and when they were 'moved on'. Fieldnotes show clients continually on the move in and around the city - women prostitutes working between King's Cross, Finsbury Park, Stamford Hill and Euston, and rent boys working between Piccadilly, Victoria, Euston and King's Cross. The problem was compounded by the possibility of the police, having observed and recognised outreach workers and their purpose, using the workers in order to locate and identify clients. In response, the style and nature of contacting strategies employed in heavily policed areas required great sensitivity, especially if they were to be conducted quickly, smoothly and effectively. As one of the workers commented, outreach workers require a "sixth sense" (w).

The team's Day and Night book, contains many fieldnotes showing that locations such as King's Cross and Piccadilly are intermittently subjected to heavy periods of policing, when women prostitutes and rent boys are 'cleaned up' and 'moved on':

"Everyone said they were either returning from the police station or had been 'troubled' by undercover police. A strange man came up to us asking 'do we know where he could get ecstasy tabs. He'd seen us giving stuff to the girls - either he was a fucking idiot or undercover" (Workers' Day and Night Book, 1990).

"Only three contacts made. Went to [name of street] first - four women were being arrested by an undercover vice officer - being led into a van. We talked to another woman about it - the police presence was great. We couldn't find anyone" (Workers' Day and Night Book, 1990).

In these circumstances, the CLASH workers were careful not to aid the police in their work:

"Women would be harassed by police if they were found with lots of condoms and lots of literature" (w).

"The women all crowded round and said that they wanted this that and the other. And the woman I was working with said 'OK, come on, come over to the bus stop' - into the bus shelter so as not to be seen. My understanding... was that if you walk away with someone, you're doing a deal... and what happened after that was immediately two women out of the group were pulled by the Old Bill, about a hundred yards away from us. They weren't arrested but they were pulled" (w).

One of the male workers had also described a similar situation in Piccadilly where they and their clients were approached by plain clothes police officers as a contact was being made:

"Whilst working on the Dilly [name of co-worker] and I had approached three or four rent boys. Then plain clothes Child Protection Section Male Vice felt our collars... took details - I had to produce my card etc..." (Workers' Day and Night Book, 1990).

These circumstances led workers to consider that they should make formal approaches to the police in order to facilitate detached contacts, and the feasibility of such a move is discussed in Chapter Seven.

Safety was of obvious concern to the outreach workers, and to ensure their safety the team had a policy of always working in pairs:

"We work in pairs for safety of the worker. On the street you're talking about arrest, you're talking about possible risk of personal injury, personal danger..." (w).

Observations in Victoria showed the ease with which outreach workers could unwittingly become involved in awkward or potentially dangerous situations. For example, a number of boys contacted at Victoria were involved in 'clipping'[5], and according to a regular rent boy contact, were best avoided:

"There's a very heavy clipping scene going on at Victoria - 20 or so young men being run by one very straight heavy man. Taking punters around the corner, taking money then hitting them..." (Workers Day and Night Book, 1990).

But the necessary methods and style of work required to work safely in such environments simply came with practice, according to one of the workers:

"When it was first done [detached work] there were lots of fears about pimps and about punters. These women live quite dangerous lives. And now we don't have to worry about that so much because the reality is of course it could happen, but unless we're really silly or unless we just stumble across something, most of the time we're dealing just purely with the women" (w).

Safety was also important in relation to the client's perception of events. For example, as one of the women workers explains when contacting women prostitutes:

"You have to remember there's a lot of other people on the streets like punters, or clients who a women might be trying to avoid or has turned down before, and she doesn't want to be trapped with you for a long period of time" (w).

Other extraneous and uncontrollable factors such as the weather, time of year or particular events also affected trade for prostitutes, and subsequently the likelihood of contacts for outreach workers. A BBC documentary programme "Operation Cottage", which concentrated on the 'cleaning up' of Victoria station's men's toilets, for example, resulted in a dramatic fall-off in trade for rent boys and simultaneously the possibility of contacts for outreach workers, while the density of tourists around Piccadilly in the summer months sometimes made conducting smooth and inconspicuous cold contacts impossible (Fieldnotes, 1990).

New clients: Characteristics

In this section we summarise the data obtained about new clients' characteristics and then go on to describe these findings as they relate to CLASH's target populations of sex industry workers and drug users.

Overview of populations reached
Figure 6.7 shows the extent to which new clients were known to be working in the sex industry (53%), to be using drugs (28%), and to be injecting drugs (22%). A further 22% were known to be living in potentially 'mobile' or 'homeless' situations, such as having 'no-fixed-abode', staying with 'friends', or living in squats, hostels and bed and breakfasts. These form the target populations which CLASH aimed to reach (see Chapter Three).

Figure 6.7   Target populations reached (N=741)

Target population*	yes	(% of n)
Women prostitutes	226	(30)
Rent boys	161	(27)
Injecting drug users	162	(22)
Other drug users	47	(6)
Homeless/mobile	146	(20)
None of the above	13	(2)
Total	755*	(—)
Not known to be above	201	(27)

* includes multiple entries (215)

In order to interpret the figures above, we need to briefly consider the extent to which those not known to be involved in prostitution (214), injecting drug use (328), or homelessness (523) were likely to be so. The probability of clients working as women prostitutes, if contacted in locations known for prostitution, can be considered to be quite high. Similarly, there is a possibility, but not necessarily a strong likelihood, that some of the boys contacted in pubs commonly frequented by rent boys, may also have been working as prostitutes but may have remained elusive about reporting such activities. It is known that rent boys in particular often deny the nature of their involvement in prostitution (Robinson, 1989), and when contacting boys on outreach sessions such 'denial' is quite common (Fieldnotes, 1989-1990). The extent to which clients not known to be using or injecting drugs were actually using or injecting is less easy to determine. It is extremely difficult to assess the likelihood of those not to known to be homeless to actually be so, in part because information about clients' living situation was for the majority of clients unknown (70%).

Where data was known about whether or not clients were involved in prostitution (527), injecting drug use (413) and living situation (218), nearly two thirds (65%) of men contacted were working as rent boys, almost all (81%) women contacted were working as prostitutes, 49% of clients were using drugs and 39% injecting, whilst 67% were in temporary or mobile accommodation. These figures include multiple entries between categories, and for example, 14% of women were involved in both prostitution and injecting drug use, as were 4% of men. Only 13 new clients were known not to be in any of these categories. Of these, four clients were known to be working as maids to women prostitutes working from flats, two had financial problems (were begging), one sought advice regarding HIV risks from anal sex, and one requested an HIV antibody test. While recognising that the target group status of a relatively high proportion of clients (27%) was unknown, CLASH can nonetheless be considered to have effectively reached their intended target groups (see Chapter Seven).

Contact with other agencies
Of the new clients contacted, 20% were known to be in current contact with other health or helping services, 21% were known not to be in contact, whilst for 59% of clients this information was not known. For those where this information was unknown, the likelihood is that they were *not* in contact with services, particularly statutory based ones. This suggests that CLASH were successful in achieving their objective of reaching out-of-contact or hard-to-reach clients (see Chapter Seven).

Of the clients in contact with agencies (148), more were in contact with the Soho Project than any other agency (42%). Others included the Cleveland Street syringe exchange (18%), the Hungerford Drug Project (16%), James Pringle House (8%), Streetwise Youth (6%) and Praed Street Clinic (6%). Current contact with agencies other than these (4%) included minimal contact with City Roads, the Caravan syringe exchange, Centre Point Night Shelter[6], the Health Improvement Team (HIT)[7], the Basement Project, Margaret Pyke Women's Health Centre[8], the Angel Project[9], the Terrence Higgins Trust, Rufford Street and Greek Street[10] hostels, and University College Hospital Casualty and DDU. Very few new clients, therefore, were in contact with statutory based agencies at the point of first contact with the CLASH team, and of those who were, the majority were in contact with the syringe exchange - a street based shop-front agency, which is noted for its 'user-friendly' and accessible approach to attracting drug users (Hart *et al.*, 1990).

As would be expected, particular client populations were likely to be in contact with particular agencies: drug injectors with Cleveland Street and Caravan syringe exchange projects, the Hungerford, City Roads and HIT, women prostitutes with the Praed Street clinic and James Pringle House, and rent boys with Streetwise and the Soho Project. Of those in contact, there were considerably less female clients in contact with agencies other than CLASH than there were male clients (20% as opposed to 50%). This trend was also true, but to a lesser degree, for women prostitutes as opposed to rent boys (37% as opposed to 46% in contact).

Clients involved in prostitution

Figure 6.8 Prostitution, drug use and homelessness

	women prostitutes	rent boys	total in sex industry
totals	226	161	387
of which			
drug users	51	47	98
injecting	47	15	62
homeless	11	51	62

Of clients known to be working in the sex industry (387), 58% (226) were working as women prostitutes, and 42% (161) as rent boys. The great majority of both rent boys and women prostitutes (86%) contacted were described by the team as 'White British', with only 6% as 'Black British', and the remaining clients as 'White European', 'Irish', or 'Asian'. Where information was known (99), almost all clients working as prostitutes lived in London or surrounding areas (90%), whilst women prostitutes appeared more likely to be commuting from outside areas than rent boys. Data relating to accommodation was unknown for the majority of women prostitutes (184) and for just under half of rent boys (71). Where this information was known (132), however, clients working as rent boys were significantly more likely to be living in temporary accommodation such as squats, hostels or to be of 'no fixed abode' than women prostitutes.

Nearly two thirds (63%) of new contacts with women prostitutes were with women working in the King's Cross area, 30% were made with women working from flats in Soho, and the remaining 7% were contacted at CLASH (4%), at Stamford Hill, at Victoria, at Piccadilly, or at a needle exchange. Women prostitutes contacted in street locations were on average younger than women working from flats in Soho (22 years as opposed to 26 years, SD=5.0 and 7.0 respectively, range 14 years to 51 years).

The average duration of new contacts with women prostitutes was ten minutes (SD=6.9, range two to 37 minutes), and contacts were considerably shorter at street locations than those made at flats (average of seven minutes as opposed to eleven minutes). As indicated by the following comments from one of the workers who was involved in setting up the King's Cross detached work, there was a clear sense of having to hurry through contacts:

"King's Cross was very threatening. It's not a very nice place to work... and I mean obviously the whole issue of police harassment was very pertinent at King's Cross and you had to be particularly sensitive to it; and also particularly sensitive to the fact that the women were working, and that if they were talking to us then a punter could be driving past or walking past, and she would lose the chance of that punter. So any exchange we had we felt had to be very fast" (w).

As a consequence, the nature of the outreach contact at women prostitutes' flats was quite different to those on the streets:

"At King's Cross we're seeing a transient population, we're seeing people being busted and arrested in front of our eyes. The people are a lot more cautious, they're less willing to stand up and talk to you and stuff like that... With the flats, you're going into closed environments, you're going into people's flats... people are more in their underwear and body stockings, whereas on the streets they're clothed. The population in the flats are normally steady people... so you're guaranteed to see the same people over and over again. They instantly recognise you, you have names like 'the condom lady'... if you meet the people in King's Cross again you'll be lucky" (w).

Most rent boys (59%) were contacted in Soho, almost all (92%) in a 'rent boy' pub. Those contacted in Piccadilly (26%) were mostly contacted on the streets (88%), whilst the remainder (15%) were contacted at Victoria station, King's Cross, Earls Court, at CLASH and at other agencies. The average street contact with rent boys was of a slightly longer duration than street contacts with women prostitutes (ten minutes as opposed to seven minutes), although there was little difference between the duration of contacts with rent boys contacted in street locations as opposed to pubs (ten minutes as opposed to eleven minutes respectively). Rent boys were on average slightly younger than women prostitutes (20 years, SD=3.7, range 14 years to 40 years; compared with 23 years), and there was no difference in age between rent boys contacted in street locations as opposed to pub locations. This can largely be explained by the fact that the same boys frequently move between street and pub locations (Fieldnotes, 1990).

Clients involved in drug use

Figure 6.9 Drug use, prostitution and homelessness

	injecting	non injecting	total
drug users	162	47	209
of which no. are			
sex industry	62	36	98
homeless	30	17	47

Of the clients who were known to be using illicit drugs (209), 63% were male and 37% female (significant difference), with a mean average age of 23 years (SD=5.7, range 14 to 47). Where data relating to drug users' living situation were available (91), most did not have secure accommodation, but instead lived in squats (36%), hostels (9%), or were of no fixed abode (34%). Almost all (95%) lived in London or surrounding areas, and where known (90), 89% were unemployed.

Approximately three quarters (77%) of the clients known to be using drugs were also known to be injecting. As with clients using drugs, there was a significant difference in the degree to which male clients injected as opposed to female clients. Clients injecting drugs were on average older than clients using but not injecting drugs: 24 years (SD=5.9, range 16 years to 47 years) as opposed to 19 years (SD=3.6, range 14 years to 30 years). The direction of age differences between injectors and non-injectors and the average age of clients involved in both injecting and non-injecting drug use reported here are consistent with other similar studies (McKeganey *et al.*, 1989; Klee *et al.*, 1990). Similarly, the direction of client gender differences are in keeping with other studies of injecting drug use (for example, Power *et al.*, 1988; McKeganey *et al.*, 1989), but the proportion of women in this sample may be considered particularly high. This can be explained by the locations targeted: for example, half (47%) of the women clients and over half of drug injectors (57%) were contacted in the King's Cross area, an area targeted primarily for contacting women prostitutes. The remaining drug injectors were contacted at a syringe exchange (21%), in Soho (8%), at CLASH (11%), at other projects (2%) and in Victoria and Piccadilly.

Outreach workers tended to express more reservations regarding the contacting of drug users and drug injectors than clients working as prostitutes. As one of the women workers explains:

"I find it a bit hard to judge people's attitudes, especially if they're users, because you don't know what they're going to be like until you start talking to them. I've contacted people in King's Cross who are users and said 'do you want works?' and they've told me just to get the fuck out of their face" (w).

Clients involved in prostitution and drug use
Where sex industry workers' drug use was known to outreach workers (244), approximately half of rent boys (46%; 47) and a third of women prostitutes (36%; 51) were known to be using illicit drugs. There was, however, a significant difference in the degree to which the two groups were injecting. Of the clients where data relating to injecting drug use was obtained (240), almost a third of women prostitutes (33%; 47) compared with 15% (15) of rent boys were injecting drugs. Although comparable data from other similar outreach projects in the UK is as yet limited, the proportion of women prostitutes contacted known also to be injecting (33%) is slightly greater than in Birmingham (25%) (Kinnell, 1989a) or Edinburgh (28%) (Morgan Thomas *et al.*, 1989), but similar to that in Liverpool (32%) (Marland Quarterly Surveillance Reports, 1989-1990). Research focusing on rent boys is even more limited, and at the time of writing there are no comparable data from rent boys contacted through outreach work. However, in the findings from a recent ethnographic study of rent boys using 'cottages' in Glasgow, there were only few reports of injecting drug use (Bloor *et al.*, 1990). Similarly, in a small London based study of street and escort/agency rent boys there was little evidence of injecting drug use (Robinson, 1989). Reports of injecting drug use among rent boys in this study are therefore greater than otherwise previously reported. This may be because rent boys contacted through outreach work may be more likely to report their injecting drug use than might have been the case had they been contacted for research purposes. This is probably largely because needles and syringes were mentioned as one of the services available to clients on most contacts, often before clients had identified themselves as injecting.

Where drug users' involvement in prostitution was known (162), as many as 60% of drug users were involved in prostitution activities: near half of male drug users, and over two thirds of female drug users. It is likely that the extent to which female and male drug users in this sample appear to be involved in prostitution is skewed due to the particular locations where contacts are made, and the team's emphasis on contacting clients involved in prostitution rather than those specifically involved in drug use.

HIV transmission behaviour
The extent to which the sex industry workers and drug injectors contacted by CLASH could be considered vulnerable to HIV infection is difficult to determine. This arose both from the brevity of the outreach contact and the nature of establishing new contacts, where the information gathered was often limited. It is possible to make only tentative statements about clients' vulnerability to HIV and other health problems as a result of their sexual and drug using behaviour.

For the majority of clients (87%) information about condom use with sexual partners was unknown. Where data were available (83; 13%) over half of the clients (52%) were thought to be using condoms 'usually' with their sexual partners, 21% 'always', and 28% 'never'. There was little difference between women prostitutes' and rent boys' reported condom use with sexual partners.

The frequency of condom use with punters was known only for 37% of those clients known to be exchanging sex for money (142). Of these, women prostitutes were likely to use condoms significantly more often with punters than rent boys. For example, 74% of women prostitutes were thought to be using condoms 'always' with punters compared with 36% of rent boys, while 26% of women prostitutes used condoms 'sometimes' with punters compared with 64% of rent boys. In other outreach studies, this overall figure is slightly higher: similar proportions of women prostitutes (63%) and rent boys (62%) 'always' used condoms in Edinburgh (Morgan Thomas *et al.*, 1989), whilst women prostitutes in Birmingham report 91% condom use during vaginal sex (Kinnell, 1989b).

Prostitute clients who used drugs were slightly less likely to use condoms with punters than prostitutes who did not use drugs. Less than half (46%) of the drug using prostitutes 'always' used condoms with punters compared with 65% of non-drug using prostitutes. Similar data emerges from studies of street working prostitutes in San Francisco and New York (Day, 1988; Carballo and Rezza, 1990). The finding that women prostitutes were less likely to be using condoms regularly with partners as opposed to punters (for example, 35% 'always' compared with 74%) is supported in the findings of recent work undertaken by Day and Ward (1990) with women prostitutes in London attending the Praed Street clinic in Paddington.

Information on clients' condom use alone tells us little about their vulnerability to HIV infection and other STDs. In answer to a question about 'other safer sex', however, data was only available for 8% (56) of new clients. Of these, the majority (59%) were thought to have 'other safer sex' 'usually', 32% 'always' and the remaining 9% 'never'. The majority of clients for whom this information was known were working as prostitutes (80%). The safer sexual activities most frequently reported were fellatio and masturbation.

Approximately half (49%) of the rent boys contacted were known to have sex exclusively with men, and 19% were known to have sex also with women. For the remainder (32%), this information was not known. These proportions are not too dissimilar from those reported by Roberson in a study of street rent boys contacted in similar London locations (Robinson, 1989). For 92% of women prostitutes this information was unknown, and so no inferences can be drawn. Of male drug injectors (94), 21% were known to have sex with men and 28% were known to have sex with women (58% and 66% unknown respectively), whilst of women drug injectors (68), 79% were known to have sex with men and under 2% to have sex with women (18% and 85% unknown respectively).

Of the clients known to be using drugs (28%), approximately three quarters (77%) were injecting. Of those injecting, only 4% (7) were known by outreach workers to be also sharing injecting equipment, all of whom were male and one of whom was HIV antibody positive. 16% were known not to be sharing, and for 80% this information was not known.

Where it was known whether or not clients had been tested for HIV antibody (90; 12%), 25% had tested antibody positive, 19% had tested antibody negative, 9% had been tested with the results unknown at the time, and 47% had yet to be tested. Of the twenty-three clients reporting a positive antibody status, twenty-one were male and two were female. Of the men, eight were working as rent boys, eight were injecting drugs, three were working as rent boys and injecting drugs, and two were using but not injecting drugs. Of the women, both were non-prostitutes and non-drug users, although one had a past history of injecting drug use. While these figures are small in number, they nevertheless are supported as a general trend elsewhere: there is little evidence in the UK currently linking seropositivity to women working as prostitutes who do not inject drugs (Day, 1988; Johnson, 1988; Morgan Thomas *et al.*, 1989).

Conversely, despite missing data, this may support findings from elsewhere which point to the possibility of higher risks being associated with the rent scene (Van den Hoek *et al.*, 1988; Tomlinson, 1991; McKeganey *et al.*, 1990).

New clients: Services provided

Condoms and works
In terms of the main street risk reduction services offered by the CLASH team, condoms were distributed to almost all women prostitutes (92%), most rent boys (73%), and half (49%) of drug injectors. The condoms supplied varied according to client need. On detached sessions with women prostitutes, condoms designed specifically for use with vaginal sex (a selection, including non-allergic and non-reservoir), a small supply of extra strength condoms (for example, 'Mates Tough' or 'HT Special') and condoms for oral use (for example, 'Durex Featherlite') were carried. On detached sessions with rent boys, condoms more suitable for anal sex ('HT Special') and condoms for oral use ('Durex Featherlite') were carried. The numbers of condoms distributed also varied according to the nature of detached contact. When working with women prostitutes based in flats, sometimes as many as one gross of condoms (135 condoms) were supplied, whereas when working with street women prostitutes and rent boys, usually no more than 20 per contact were given. As one of the workers indicated, the opportunities provided by street locations for the provision of outreach services were likely to be more restricted than environments such as cafes, pubs or client's flats:

> "It's very different on the streets. With the flats its easier because you can tell them about all of the services, but on the street you have such limited time that you really can't go into it all. So if a woman don't really want to know she wants to get her clients, and time is money" (w).

Just under a fifth of women prostitutes (18%) were also provided with lubricants, as were 23% of rent boys, and 12% of women were provided with spermicide. Three-quarters (75%) of drug injectors were also provided with clean works. Clean injecting equipment was distributed in 'works packs' - pre-wrapped bags of mixed or single-type works - typically, a 'mixed bag' containing five one ml, three two and a half ml and three five ml syringe barrels, a selection of needle sizes (for drawing up and injecting), swabs, one packet of 'HT Special' condoms, and a selection of agency/syringe exchange cards. Over a third (36%) of clients were provided with a 'CLASH card' detailing risk reduction services offered and contact numbers. Other services provided included the provision of counselling advice, latex gloves, health education literature, and bleach.

Issues discussed
The following data are based on questions regarding the nature of issues discussed with clients on outreach contacts. Where indicated, issues relating to sexuality and sexual behaviour were discussed with 16% of clients, drug related issues with 11%, STDs with 12%, other medical issues with 7%, and other non-medical issues with 8%.

Of the new clients who were involved in discussions about sexuality and sexual behaviour (119), 73% (87) of clients discussed the use of condoms with their punters, and 34% (41) with their sexual partners. Other safer sexual activities were only discussed with 14% (17) of clients, where most discussion centred around oral sex. Specific risks to HIV transmission through sexual behaviour were discussed with 31% (37) of clients, and most advice related to risks associated with anal sex and oral sex.

A variety of issues were covered with the clients (78) with whom drug use was discussed, each with approximately a fifth of clients (11-17): disposing of dirty works, cleaning works, sharing works, getting a detox, getting a script, stopping fixing, and use of alcohol. Other discussions covered issues relevant to particular drugs such as heroin, amphetamines and temazepan, finding safer injecting sites, and general discussions about the extent of clients' drug use.

With the discussions relating to STDs (85), most (with 43%; 37 clients) involved advice as to where to get appropriate help, 33% (28) were concerned with particular STDs, 28% (24) were concerned with advice about HIV antibody testing, and 14% (12) were concerned specifically with hepatitis.

Of discussions involving other medical issues (48), 52% (25) were about gynaecological issues, and 14% involved advising clients where to get help regarding particular medical problems. Of further non-medical discussions (58), 38% (22) related to clients' relationships, 29% (17) to housing problems, and 22% (13) to legal problems. Other issues discussed included problems with the police, social security, money, and nutrition.

Further contact and referral
CLASH made specific arrangements for further contact with 13% (94) of new clients. Only a quarter (23%) of these were formal appointments at the CLASH office, whilst the remainder (77%) were agreements for clients to phone back, call back in person or to come to the Friday morning drop-in service. The reasons for arranging further contact were varied, but most commonly mentioned were in order to establish the contact, to provide a further supply of condoms or works, to simply have a chat or to give advice, to talk about the possibilities for HIV antibody testing, or to discuss clients' HIV transmission risks and safer sex, clients' drug use or clients' involvement with prostitution.

Referrals to other agencies were made with 12% (92) of new clients. Of these referrals, the majority were to statutory based organisations: 36% (33) of clients were referred to James Pringle House at the Middlesex Hospital, 12% (11) to the Cleveland Street syringe exchange, 11% (10) to the Health Improvement Team (HIT) at the National Temperance Hospital, and 10% (9) to the Margaret Pyke Women's Health Centre at the Soho Hospital. As one of the workers pointed out:

> "We know we can refer to JPH and we know there's good doctors there, and we know we can refer to the needle exchange. There are certain places we know" (w).

Other less common referrals to statutory based organisations included those to University College Hospital casualty and drug dependency clinic, Praed Street clinic at St. Mary's Hospital, and Guy's Hospital STD clinic. The minority of referrals were to non-statutory based organisations: 6% (6) to the Basement Youth Project, 6% (6) to the Soho Project, 6% (6) to the Hungerford Drug Project, 5% (5) to City Roads, and 5% (5) to the Terrence Higgins Trust. Other less common referrals to non-statutory based organisations included referrals to Streetwise Youth, Positively Women, Rathbone Place Hostel, and various other hostels and night shelters.

In interpreting these data it must be clear what constitutes a referral. In over half of the referrals (55%) clients were given only verbal instruction, whilst for a third of referrals (36%) the appropriate agency was also phoned. Other arrangements were made in 9% of cases, and these included accompanying clients to the referral destination, making arrangements with particular referral agency staff, and facilitating the ease and speed of referral appointments by instructing the client to show a CLASH card on arrival to the referral destination.

Reported reasons for client referral were varied, but of the reasons specified, some broad areas became apparent: for drug related problems (10), for general medical check-up (10), for gynaecological concerns (7), for HIV related problems (4), for STDs (3), for housing (2), for legal (2) and for contraception (2).

An assessment of referral outcome in relation to total clients referred can be found below, and discussion regarding the achievement of referral objectives in Chapter Seven.

Re-contacted clients: Characteristics

The majority (96%) of the 642 re-contacts were face to face contacts, with only 3% made by telephone and under 1% through client letters. Re-contacts were more likely than new contacts to be client initiated (38% as opposed to 11%), with 60% of re-contacts being CLASH initiated and the remainder (2%) initiated through other projects. The average duration of the re-contact was slightly shorter than the new contact: 11 minutes (SD=13.4, range 1 minute to 130 minutes) compared with 13 minutes (SD=15.5, range 1 minute to 180 minutes). Subsequent street based re-contacts with clients were on average slightly longer.

Slightly fewer of client re-contacts (81%) than new contacts were detached outreach contacts. Of these (519), over half (55%) were contacts in women prostitutes' flats, 39% were street contacts, and the remaining 6% were made in pubs and cafes. Of the non-detached contacts (123), most (70%) were located in the CLASH office or at other projects, such as the Hungerford Project, Cleveland Street syringe exchange, University College Hospital, and James Pringle House at the Middlesex Hospital.

Target populations re-contacted
Unlike on first contact, the majority of the 188 clients re-contacted were female (72%), while the average age of clients was the same as on new contact (23 years; range 14 to 55 years). Where information was known (23), seven of the re-contacted clients (all male) were known to be HIV antibody positive, five were known to be antibody negative (four women), seven had yet to be tested, while one was awaiting test results.

Figure 6.10 below summarises the extent to which target populations were re-contacted. Of the 188 clients re-contacted, and on the basis of the information known at the point of first (new) contact, 56% (105) were known to be working as women prostitutes, 9% (17) to be working as rent boys, and 25% to be injecting drugs. These figures include multiple entries between categories, and as the figure below shows, 10% (18) of re-contacted clients were both working as women prostitutes and injecting drugs, and 2% (4) were both working as rent boys and injecting drugs. The most notable variation between clients at first and re-contact was the increased likelihood of contacting women prostitutes on re-contacts (56% as opposed to 30%), and the corresponding decrease in the contacting of rent boys (9% as opposed to 22%). The extent to which drug injectors were contacted was similar: 25% at the point of re-contact and 22% at first contact.

Figure 6.10 Target population re-contacted

total recontacts	188		
of which			
		male	female
prostitution		17	105
injecting drugs		23	25
prostitutes injecting			
drugs		4	18

The increased tendency to re-contact women prostitutes over and above other target groups was also reflected in the way in which the total number of re-contacts (642) (as opposed to the total number of clients re-contacted [188]) were divided between the target groups. For example, while 56% of the clients re-contacted were known to be women prostitutes, 67% of total re-contacts were made with this client group. Thus the average number of re-contacts made with women prostitutes was four (with a median of four, and a range of 1-25), while rent boys were re-contacted a median average of two times (mean average of four is skewed owing to atypical contact with one client involving 25 re-contacts), as were drug injectors (range 1-10).

The increased rate of re-contact with women prostitutes was a factor largely determined by location of outreach contact. The distribution of re-contacts between those made with women prostitutes on the street in King's Cross and those made in women's flats in Soho, highlights this difference. Although the total number of clients contacted in each of these locations is similar, the average number of re-contacts per client contacted at the Soho flats is greater than that in King's Cross - five times (range 1 to 23) as opposed to slightly under three (range 1 to 8). As mentioned earlier, despite occasional personnel changes, flat workers are by comparison a relatively stable population: "a sitting population rather than a moving population" (w), and thus more accessible to outreach contact:

> "The women that we made contact with (at Soho flats) very quickly became very trusting of us. You know, the initial thing was like 'who the hell are these people?' and we obviously had to make it apparent very quickly that we weren't police and we weren't wanting anything from them, but they kind of cottoned onto it very fast, and I think they felt quite... good about the fact that somebody was actually coming round... We made it a regular Thursday afternoon slot. And we got quite friendly with them. I mean, they ended up giving us presents - we would get royal jelly given to us and we'd get stockings given to us" (w).

So, of new clients involved in female prostitution (226), male prostitution (161) and injecting drug use (162), just under half (46%) of women prostitutes were re-contacted, 11% of rent boys and 30% of drug injectors. It is clear that the CLASH project's target population least likely to be re-contacted, especially over time, was rent boys. It is also evident that CLASH effectively made re-contact with their target populations: 83% of women contacted were known to be working as women prostitutes or injecting drugs (or both), while 69% of men were working as rent boys or injecting drugs (or both).

In an attempt to gain some measure of effectiveness of the outreach contact, it is necessary to consider the extent to which clients' behaviour changed over time. In practice, however, this became a very crude exercise, partly because the average number of re-contacts per client were relatively low, but mainly because the information required was unavailable to outreach workers. This problem is further compounded by the fact that different outreach workers often re-contacted the same client over time, and the state of their knowledge about client behaviour often differed between each other. In this context, even if change had noticeably occurred, it would be extremely difficult to gain a reliable or valid indicator as to whether or not that change was attributable to the CLASH intervention.

In practice, there were few changes which did occur between clients' behaviour on first and re-contact and within re-contacts themselves.

Figure 6.11 below shows the behaviours in which re-contacted clients were engaging at the point of last re-contact. When compared to Figure 6.10 above, which shows these details as they were at the point of first contact, it is clear the differences are minimal.

Figure 6.11 Clients at last re-contact

total recontacts	188	
of which		
	male	female
prostitution	22 (+5)	107 (-2)
injecting drugs	22 (-1)	26 (+1)
prostitutes injecting		
drugs	4 (-)	18 (-)

figures in brackets denote change between first and last contact

The changes which did occur between first and last contact can be summarised as follows. On the one hand, four clients stopped injecting (two of which were women prostitutes), one female injector stopped working as a prostitute, and one male client stopped working as a rent boy. On the other hand, one women prostitute started injecting, and three men started working as rent boys. Furthermore, information which was previously unknown to outreach workers became known over time: two women prostitutes were confirmed to be drug injectors, three women became known to be working as prostitutes, one man to be working as a rent boy, one female injector to be working as a prostitute, and two male injectors to be working as rent boys.

Re-contacted clients: Services provided

On three-quarters of re-contacts (75%) condoms were distributed, in almost all cases to clients working as prostitutes. Packs of works were distributed on 17% of re-contacts, lubricants on 28%, spermicide on 11%, and a CLASH card on 13%. Other services provided (where specified) mostly included the provision of counselling (14), or of advice and information (8).

Further contact and referral

Arrangements for further contact with the CLASH team were arranged on 17% of re-contacts. In a third of such cases (33%) arrangements involved making an appointment at the CLASH office. In most cases (66%) other arrangements were made, where the client would agree to phone back or drop-in. The specified reasons for making further arrangements for re-contact with clients were many and varied: for counselling, sometimes HIV related (28), to make arrangements or to discuss the possibility of referral elsewhere (27), to simply make a regular visit possible or to further establish a client relationship (18), or to collect works or condoms (11). Other less common reasons mentioned included advice regarding STDs, mental health, drug use, and involvement in prostitution.

Arrangements for further contact were therefore made 110 times (17% of re-contacts) with 40 clients: an average of almost three arrangements per re-contacted client. To assess the efficiency of these arrangements, not only do we have to consider the proportion of clients further re-contacted where arrangements had been made, but also the proportion of clients re-contacted where there were no such arrangements. Of the 110 contacts where arrangements for further contact were made, 85 subsequent re-contacts occurred and 28 clients were never re-contacted. Of the remaining occasions where arrangements were not made, 347 re-contacts occurred.

At a glance, these figures seem to suggest that it is far more likely for re-contacts to occur should arrangements for further contact not be made by the CLASH team. This, however, is not the case for two reasons. First, where arrangements were made this was often for something specific and usually involved the client making an appointment at the CLASH project. Under these circumstances, that the team achieved a 75% success rate for positive returns out of the 110 arrangements they made can be considered very encouraging. In contrast, it is far less surprising that clients should be re-contacted in regular outreach locations, whether with or without specific arrangements. Second, the team's success rate can be considered perhaps even more of an achievement when noting that thirteen of the 28 clients who were never re-contacted once arrangements had been made, were re-contacted in the first instance in the two months prior to data collection being completed. It may not be unreasonable to expect that these clients will be contacted again in the future.

Arrangements for referral to agencies other than CLASH were made with 39 clients, on 64 occasions (10% of re-contacts). Of these clients, the majority (21) were women prostitutes, one was a rent boy, six were drug injectors, six were women prostitutes and drug injectors, four were non prostitute, non drug injecting men and one was a non prostitute, non injecting woman.

Of the 64 separate referrals made, most were to statutory based organisations: 47% (30) to James Pringle House, 11% (7) to Praed Street Clinic at St. Mary's Hospital, 8% (5) to City Roads Crisis Intervention Centre, and 6% (4) to Cleveland Street syringe exchange. The remainder of referrals included referrals to the Health Improvement Team, Oak Lodge Hostel, Mainliners, the Hungerford Drug Project, the Soho Project and other hostels.

In over half (56%) of these referrals the appropriate agency was first telephoned by the CLASH team, on 24% of occasions clients were given verbal instruction, and on the remaining occasions other arrangements were made, which included accompanying clients to their referral destination and allowing clients to arrange their own referrals by phone or by letter.

The reasons for client referrals specified included those drug related (10), those for gynaecological checks (7), for general medical check ups (7), for housing advice/assistance (5), for counselling (3), and for HIV test advice/results (2).

In order to provide some measure of referral outcome, two of the agencies to which clients were commonly referred (James Pringle House at Middlesex Hospital and the Health Improvement Team) were asked to keep a basic record of CLASH referrals. Other agencies, such as Cleveland Street syringe exchange and voluntary agencies, do not systematically collect the information required or held such information confidential. The contact sheet data for new clients cited above indicates a total of 33 clients referred to James Pringle House and 10 to the Health Improvement Team. The re-contact sheet data for established clients indicates a total of 30 clients referred to James Pringle House and 3 to the Health Improvement Team, giving a total of 63 referrals to James Pringle House and 13 to the Health Improvement Team. In practice, James Pringle House were able only to keep records after data collection had been completed (where ten clients were seen a total of eighteen times over the six month period July to December 1990). It is thought by the doctor responsible for recording CLASH referrals at JPH that the number of positive outcomes from CLASH referrals to JPH (i.e.. the client arrives at JPH) are under 20%. Since January 1988, the Health Improvement Team recorded a total of three referrals from CLASH, two involving client telephone calls, and one involving a client in person accompanied by one of the CLASH workers. This gives a success rate of 23%.

The CLASH team themselves were also asked to record the outcome of previous referrals with re-contacted clients. Of the 64 referrals made, 24 were known by CLASH to have been successful, 17 were known not to have been successful, and for 23 the referral outcome was unknown. This gives a 37% success rate.

It must be stressed that there are few reliable quantitative indicators of the efficacy of referral, apart from the impressions noted above. The likelihood is that the 37% success rate for referrals of re-contacted clients noted by the CLASH team is an over-estimate. Certainly, the experiences of those working in the project's main referral points would seem to suggest this. This is considered in Chapter Seven, where we discuss the evaluation of referral objectives, drawing on the wealth of qualitative data available.

CHAPTER SEVEN

EVALUATING OUTREACH CONTACT AND SERVICE DELIVERY

Drawing on the findings presented in Chapter Six, we discuss the evaluation of the CLASH project in the light of project service delivery and development. As will become clear, the tensions existing between participants on these aspects of project work were inextricably linked with those concerned with management. Just as we have considered the efficacy of the management process in terms of the objectives of the management structure to facilitate a collaboration between voluntary and statutory managers, here we consider the effectiveness of the project's outreach work in the light of project aims and objectives. In doing this, we address two points. First we consider the differing viewpoints and perceptions of outreach service delivery and objectives which existed between CLASH workers and voluntary and statutory managers; and second, we consider the criteria by which such a service should be evaluated.

As reported in Chapter Three, CLASH defined their project objectives as principally: to contact those not accessing health services, including the young homeless, drug users, and women and men working as prostitutes; to train workers in existing voluntary projects (not formally evaluated); to provide and facilitate referrals to other health services, voluntary organisations and social services; and to provide clients with appropriate health education, advice, counselling, condoms and injecting equipment. In evaluating the extent to which CLASH have achieved these objectives, the following discussion is divided into three sections: detached client contact; facilitating access to services; and supply of, and demand for, outreach services. We then go on to consider the wider issues of outreach service development, and the role that outreach might play in the future prevention of HIV infection.

Hard to reach or out of reach?: Detached client contact

In the period 1st January 1988 to 31st July 1990, the CLASH team recorded a total of 1383 separate outreach contacts with 741 different clients. This gives an average of 45 contacts per month, with proportionately greater numbers of clients, both new and established, being contacted throughout the first seven months of 1990.

A number of factors have to be examined when attempting to make an assessment of these figures in the light of the team's objectives to reach the hard-to-reach. First, what amount of contact might have been expected of the project; second, to what extent were the clients contacted actually hard-to-reach, in terms of having little or no contact with existing services; and third, were the clients contacted drawn from the appropriate target populations? The wider question of the effectiveness of these contacts in terms of health education and prevention depends upon a variety of outcomes, such as further contact, referral, service delivery, and client health behaviour, and will be considered throughout this chapter as a whole.

Perceptions and expectations
As we have seen, there were differing perceptions of the CLASH project's objectives among the critical actors involved. This inevitably meant that differing critical actors had differing expectations of what the CLASH project should achieve in the light of its stated objectives. The extent of client contact was no exception. According to one member of the Steering Group this issue was "at the heart of the difference" between voluntary and statutory representatives. One of the voluntary managers described how he viewed the Health Authority's perception of detached and outreach work:

"The Health Authority managers might understand - 'Oh yes, this is exciting innovative work, it needs to be done, it's at the cutting edge of streetwork and it's at the cutting edge of HIV intervention' but what they don't understand is that it takes a year or eighteen months to establish and to really firmly establish in terms of direct face to face work" (v).

This would imply that one should not attempt to assess the work of CLASH until the project had established itself with regular working patterns - a process which, in the experience of the above voluntary manager, could take well over a year. But some of the statutory representatives, contrary to the expectations of some voluntary managers, did seem aware of the time required to establish outreach work, recognising that:

"It was difficult and frightening to really set out on the streets and set people up, and very difficult to know how to approach some of these people" (s).

"It's actually very difficult to develop outreach work, and that a two year lead in time is not unusual" (s).

"Some of their outreach work and streetwork...is a lot more difficult than people with no experience of it like me would appreciate" (s).

Of course these comments are retrospective and statutory members' views of streetwork may have changed in the light of experience with the development of the CLASH project. As one of the original workers remarked, whilst "we got into asking what it was all about for the first six months or so", "the Health Authority personnel didn't understand at all the nature of detached work". As a voluntary manager commented:

"There seemed to be an expectation from some of the Health Authority management that they would employ these workers and they would go rushing out into the streets and save lives" (v).

It now appears to be generally accepted among managers and workers alike that it can take up to two years to establish detached work in a project. Although statistics are unavailable for the first nine months of the project's history (April-December, 1987), it is encouraging to note that after the initial six months monitoring of detached work, the number of monthly contacts began to increase significantly. The number of monthly contacts made towards the end of 1989 and throughout the first seven months of 1990 followed a fairly stable pattern and were considerably greater than those of a year before.

Whilst allowing for a period of time to establish the project's detached work, the question remains as to precisely what criteria should be used to evaluate the total numbers of contacts made by the CLASH team. Despite the desires of statutory managers for a head count, community based interventions are notoriously unamenable to this approach, and there may be "no technological fix to this particular problem" (Klein and Carter, 1988). In short, the number of contacts achieved may be considered acceptable to some critical actors but not to others. In this respect, representatives from the Health Authority were probably more likely to be torn between recognising the difficulty of outreach work on the one hand and remaining concerned for 'numbers' on the other, than were representatives from the voluntary sector. As one statutory representative indicated:

"It... seems to have been so difficult to really contact people. And it may be that I'm being unfair, but certainly it's been reflected in the figures that one produces that there don't seem to be all that many contacts being made" (s).

In contrast, a voluntary representative felt that "accounting" for numbers of clients should not be the "primary aim":

"...it's a particular perception that's put on streetwork, and it probably goes to the heart of the difference to where voluntary sector involvement is seeing streetwork as opposed to where the Health Authority is seeing it. Because the Health Authority would think in terms of - if we have these people parachuted to King's Cross we can count how many working women there are... we should get increasing numbers at JPH... But if you're a streetworker going out and experiencing those working women each night, what you're trying to do is respond in a more total sense to what is needed" (v).

There was thus an uneasy ambivalence between statutory and voluntary managers' perceptions of what they expected the project to achieve. These differences - between the desire to 'account for numbers' and to achieve a certain quantity of project output and the competing desire to emphasise the quality of client contacts - were inextricably linked to managers' wider perceptions of the fundamental role of the project in delivering and providing services. This we will return to later. In the meantime, one possible approach for attempting to evaluate the extent of the project's outreach contact is to look for indicators of comparability in the performance of other similar outreach projects in the United Kingdom.

Comparisons with other UK outreach projects
In attempting to find an appropriate comparison, it must be noted that these will provide very crude indicators for a number of reasons. First, at the time of writing there are few outreach projects established in the United Kingdom for which figures are available, and which aim to contact such a wide cross-section of hard-to-reach populations as

CLASH. Second, the figures which are available, including those generated within this evaluation, will vary in their reliability and validity as indicators of the work achieved. Third, there are many regional differences relating to the extent to which particular hard-to-reach populations are contactable, and the nature of their vulnerability to HIV infection. Finally, there are many differences in terms of the level of project resources and the specific aims and objectives of interventions. Thus, comparability between figures demonstrating the extent of outreach contact will be directly influenced by factors such as the amount of outreach time invested, amount of staff and financial input, contacting strategies used, the nature and extent of health services on offer, and the objectives of particular interventions - for example - the balance between peripatetic and detached outreach work, and the balance between *in situ* health education and referral.

Outreach contact figures, and some observational and fieldwork data, are available from projects in Plymouth, Liverpool, Birmingham and Sheffield. In Plymouth, approximately 60 street working women prostitutes were contacted using a mobile outreach unit between late 1987 and mid 1989 (Roberts, 1989). Unlike the women prostitutes contacted by the CLASH team, the Plymouth women worked a defined location, most were known to each other, and most worked the same location for long periods of time, apart from occasional trips to London or Bristol (Fieldnotes, 1989). It was possible, therefore, to contact the same women over long periods of time. The service was located in the heart of the working district once a week, and allowed a space for the women to drop-in, take a break and have a chat. Observations in Plymouth showed the service to operate like a 'union', allowing an opportunity for the women to work collectively: to discuss prices and services offered, to check whether new or unknown workers were undercutting prices or offering unsafe sex and so on (Fieldnotes, 1989). Responses would be formulated and action agreed, and in this way, the outreach unit provided the women with an opportunity to create a safer, more supportive working environment. The police were co-operative and allowed the women to work free from police harassment, in some cases actually preventing harassment from dangerous or awkward punters.

In Liverpool, outreach services are co-ordinated and monitored on a Region-wide basis by Mersey RHA's Drugs and HIV Monitoring Unit. The outreach services are split into three separate sections of teams working exclusively with working women, rent boys and drug injectors (Fieldnotes, 1990). As far as contacts with women prostitutes are concerned, in the two year period January 1989 to December 1990, a total of 311 women prostitutes were contacted a total of 3268 times (a mean average per client of ten times) by two full-time outreach workers (Maryland Centre Quarterly Surveillance Reports, 1989-1990). The extent of outreach contact in Liverpool with women prostitutes is approximately five times that of CLASH's over a slightly longer period (26 months [started in May 1988, data collection finished in July 1990] as opposed to 24) with similar levels of staffing: CLASH contacted 226 women prostitutes a total of 658 times. The rate of re-contact in Liverpool (which has been calculated as an average per all clients contacted rather than those re-contacted) is approximately five times greater than with CLASH's clients (ten as opposed to two times).

The CLASH project's rate of new client contact with rent boys compares slightly more favourably with the Liverpool figures. Liverpool data is available over the nine month period January to September 1990 (outreach with rent boys ended in October 1989), where a total of 33 rent boys were contacted a total of 313 times (an average of nine times each) by one half time outreach worker (Maryland Centre Quarterly Surveillance Reports, 1989). Over a typical nine month period (January to September 1988), the CLASH project contacted a total of 57 rent boys. The average number of re-contacts per CLASH clients, however, was nearer one and a half times in contrast to Liverpool's nine and a half times. The CLASH project, at least for most of the time, also invested the equivalent of four times as much staffing time in detached work with rent boys than did Liverpool. In this respect, as with outreach contacts with women prostitutes, CLASH's rate of contact is considerably lower than that reported from Liverpool.

Three main reasons for this difference can be suggested. First, proportionately greater time is invested in detached outreach work per outreach worker by the Liverpool outreach team, and less time invested in training and peripatetic outreach work. Second, and most importantly, target populations are generally more accessible than CLASH's typically transient client groups. Outreach contacts with women prostitutes in Liverpool, for example, were nearly all (90%) made by car in one street location (known as "the Block"), where women work on a regular basis, and where the majority contacts are client initiated (Fieldnotes, 1990; Maryland Centre Quarterly Surveillance Reports, 1989-1990). This explains the much higher rate of new contact, and particularly of re-contact with women prostitutes and other clients in Liverpool than in London. Third, Mersey RHA have successfully negotiated with the police to facilitate the ease with which outreach and HIV prevention work is undertaken - for example, an agreement has been made where the police will only caution on an individual's first drug offence, and further negotiations are in progress to extend the possibilities of 'decriminalising' drug use in the Region (Newcombe, 1990).

Central Birmingham Health Authority's outreach initiative, the Safe Project, also aims to contact women working as prostitutes. Between August 1987 and June 1990 the project contacted 707 women prostitutes, and during the period April 1989 to April 1990, made a total of 3119 separate outreach contacts at various locations (Safe Project, 1990). With a similar staffing input to the CLASH project, two outreach workers target women prostitutes, and with the use of a car, work in locations where regular contacts with women could be made (Fieldnotes, 1990). The project has liaised with local police. These Birmingham figures are overall nearly four times greater than those reported by the CLASH team over a slightly shorter period (31 as opposed to 34 months): since January 1988 and July 1990, CLASH contacted 226 women prostitutes 658 times.

The Sheffield AIDS Education Project has undertaken detached outreach work with women prostitutes and rent boys since mid-1988. Data are available for the period April 1990 to November 1990. Throughout these nine months, the project made a total of 207 separate outreach contacts with 50 women prostitutes (Sheffield AIDS Education Project, 1990). This rate of contact and re-contact is similar to the CLASH project's, although CLASH were allotted approximately twice as much staffing time. On an average monthly basis the CLASH project contacted slightly greater numbers of women prostitutes than Sheffield, although both projects had the same average rate of client re-contact (average four times per re-contacted client).

As we have suggested, the opportunities for increased cold contact and re-contact with clients in each of the areas visited, largely depended on the relative transience or stability of their hard-to-reach. In this sense, the greater transience of central London's hard-to-reach - who might be termed the 'harder-to-reach' - demand a very different style of outreach work. To reach clients pocketed and moving within and across the city, where policing and surveillance seems intense by comparison, outreach workers need to develop more direct and aggressive contacting strategies. The probabilities of achieving client contacts and re-contacts will remain far lower than in other areas of the UK, and so the level of time, resources and workers invested as a function of outreach contact, far higher.

Evaluating the extent of client contact
In evaluating the extent of contact which the CLASH team have made
with clients, there is a general consensus among project managers to
have expected greater numbers. The possibility of increasing the extent
of contact with clients should not be excluded. One critical factor which
has emerged (other than the transience of target groups) is the proportion
of project time invested in detached outreach work. Two other
suggestions, which seem less critical to the level of outcome achieved,
but which might also improve the rate of contact, are liaison with police
and the increased use of indigenous outreach workers. We return to
these below.

When examining the indicators of random week timetables (RWTs)
and project diaries to elucidate how much time CLASH invested in
detached outreach work compared with peripatetic outreach, training
and other work, it becomes clear that the team invested the minority of
its time in detached work. The estimate is crude and should be
interpreted with caution, but approximately 35% of the team's typical
weekly time was allocated to undertaking detached outreach work, 4%
to undertaking peripatetic outreach and training work (for which there
are no client figures) and 9% in the client drop-in service (see Chapter
Five). Thus, under half (48%) of the team's total weekly time was
specifically allocated to client based work. Of the remaining half (52%)
of project time, 31% was allocated to management and consultancy, 7%
to visitors and other meetings, with the remainder (14%) split between
project administration, further meetings, induction and staff training.

Although varying throughout the study period, the detached work
ostensibly entailed two sessions every three weeks with women
prostitutes at King's Cross, two sessions every two to three weeks with
rent boys at Piccadilly, Soho or Victoria, and one session every week
with working women at Soho flats. The sessions lasted between three
to eight hours and usually involved two outreach workers.

Outreach projects elsewhere in the UK, however, are known to invest
proportionately greater periods of time in detached and peripatetic
outreach work. For example, in a recent survey, over half of the outreach
projects surveyed said that they invested at least 50% of their time
undertaking outreach work, and those investing greater periods of time
in detached work contacted significantly more clients (Hartnoll *et al.*,
1990; Rhodes *et al.*, 1991b). As one statutory manager of CLASH
commented: "I sense that there's very much less outreach work, actual
on-the-street contact going on, than I would like" (s).

But the proportion of the CLASH team's time actually spent doing detached and peripatetic outreach work, was probably even less than that allocated or probably anticipated. The team's RWTs, diaries and log books show that a significant minority of detached and peripatetic sessions were cancelled, postponed or re-arranged. Observations at CLASH and evaluators' fieldnotes (1989-1990) show this to be have been primarily a function of the team's decision making and time-management process. Not only had the team allocated as much project time to management as they did to undertaking detached outreach work, in practice they actually appeared to invest less time in detached outreach (16%) and client based work as a whole (27%), than they did in management (25%), other meetings (16%) and project administration (18%) (see Chapter Five).

In practice then, not only did the team devote an inordinate amount of time to the management process, they also mis-managed themselves when it came to action - when actually doing the work (see Chapter Four). For example, outreach sessions would be cancelled due to the mis-management of the team's time, which often meant that workers' time-off-in-lieu ('toil') had accumulated to the point that workers would take 'toil' rather than undertake their outreach sessions. Illness of workers had obvious and direct effects on the cancellation of detached sessions, as the team divided most work by gender, if not by sexuality, and all work was undertaken in pairs. The fairly high turnover of staff in the team, coupled with two or three monthly 'induction' periods for replacement workers, sometimes meant that incomplete or impossible combinations of workers (on the basis of gender, sexuality and so on) were available to do detached work. Lack of communication between team members further compounded the problem, and meetings and outreach sessions would sometimes be cancelled simply as a result of mis-understanding or lack of agreement. As one of the workers put it, streetwork was considered (somewhat amazingly) by team members as the "first casualty":

> "As soon as somebody is sick, as soon as someone is on holiday, as soon as the Health Authority demands that we do administration or write papers on this that and the other, the first thing that usually falls on its face is the streetwork" (w).

So although the principal "problem of outreach work", as described by one statutory manager, is that it requires "an awful lot of legwork for very few people", the problems of the CLASH team's outreach work went far deeper. The problem the project experienced with internal management functioning also had direct and negative consequences on the organisation of project work, and specifically, on detached outreach work - the very reason for its existence. But issues of management functioning aside, the central characteristic of outreach work which must be recognised by any institution or organisation as a pre-requisite to becoming involved in such work is that:

"You do need enormous resources to actually access people. And therefore you've got a question of whether you want to use enormous resources to pick up few people who aren't getting to any voluntary organisations or any statutory organisations" (s).

Improving detached outreach contact
Accepting outreach work as requiring "enormous resources to pick up few people" does not detract from the possibility or need for improvements to be made. We suggest three main areas of possible improvement to the CLASH team's working practices, each of which have the potential to facilitate the ease with which detached outreach contacts are made. The first of these we have discussed above, and involved the recommendation that the CLASH team should invest a greater proportion of project time to detached outreach and client-based work compared with other activities such as team management and administration. We suggest perhaps as much as 65% of total project time should be allocated to detached outreach and client-based work. We also stress that the day to day management of project time and activities is equally - if not more - important as the allocation of time alone in order to ensure that the time allocated is in practice invested. The remaining suggestions for improvement involve liaising with police and the use of indigenous outreach workers.

At the time of writing, the CLASH team have yet to liaise with police in relation to their presence in heavily policed areas and the nature and purpose of their work. The question of whether to liaise with the police, and whether this will improve working practices, is both ideological and pragmatic in nature.

There are distinct practical advantages in liaising with the police, as long as there are clear assurances that they can be trusted not to disrupt or interfere in the undertaking of outreach work. Perhaps the main concern of outreach workers is that they should not unwittingly assist the police in the identification of prostitutes and drug users. But this alone cannot be seen as a sufficient reason to avoid liaison. While undertaking participant observations in Victoria it was clear that the police were aware of the CLASH workers' presence, their purpose in being there and the nature of their work. In these circumstances the police could quite possibly have observed the movements of outreach workers in an attempt to pin-point people they themselves wished to target. This, however, might be considered one of the reasons to liaise, in an attempt to ensure that the police do not interfere in the undertaking of outreach work and do not identify their targets in this way. On the basis of our observations in Victoria, where there were no reported occasions of the police using outreach workers as a means to identify their own targets, and where the presence of outreach workers appeared known to the police, we feel that there is little danger in approaching the police with a view to discussing the needs and requirements of outreach work. This at least may minimise any potential police confusion about the presence of outreach workers in heavily policed areas and may facilitate the ease with which outreach workers are able to conduct contacts with clients. Whether such discussion also leads to formalising a mutually satisfiable agreement between the police and the project (as has been achieved in Liverpool and Plymouth) may be questionable, but attempts to do this should be encouraged. Such an arrangement might provide opportunities for the referral of clients contacted by the police to the CLASH team for advice and information and might also facilitate opportunities for greater police understanding of hard-to-reach clients' needs.

The possibility of liaison with police emerged within the CLASH team as a result of the increased policing of areas such as King's Cross and Piccadilly. The team, however, were yet to discuss the possibility of police liaison in any detail. One worker in particular felt there was a need for police liaison and felt that the initial contact and negotiations should involve representatives from the CLASH Steering or Management Groups (Fieldnotes, 1990). Whilst this particular worker felt that an agreement drawn between Bloomsbury outreach services and local police would facilitate the ease with which detached contacts could be made, he was also aware of other workers views' being contrary to this. For some of the CLASH workers, the very *idea* of liaising with the police was monstrous. This was a result of long standing mistrust, personal avoidance or just plain dislike of the police, coupled with a belief that if clients ever knew liaison had occurred, they would see this as collusive and threatening. While our observations have indeed shown that the building of trust between worker and client is an important, as well as sometimes delicate and lengthy process, we feel confident that most clients would understand both the nature of police liaison and its purpose. This would especially be the case, if (as elsewhere) liaison resulted in visible benefits both for the team's outreach work and their clients.

The second suggestion for improvement to working practices is the use of indigenous outreach workers - that is, former or current prostitutes or drug users. This practice is rather less common in the UK than in the United States (Rhodes *et al.*, 1990b), although is not without its problems (Rhodes *et al.*, 1991a; Friedman *et al.*, 1990). The use of indigenous outreach workers, however, has been shown to facilitate the ease with clients are contacted and the impact of health recommendations communicated (Wiebel, 1988; McAuliffe *et al.*, 1987; Feeney *et al.*, 1989).

Within the CLASH team, there have been two full-time workers with direct experience of either drug use or sex industry work. At one time the team made attempts to employ an indigenous sessional worker but this was unsuccessful (see Chapter Three). As one of the workers with personal experience of the rent scene explained:

"I don't think it is essential, but it gives an extra cutting edge to the work. It enables that worker to have an overview and an understanding that perhaps another worker would not have. But I think that can also be gained by talking in a very open way with the people that have got that experience" (w).

This latter point was confirmed by one of the workers without such experience:

"People's direct experience can be of value to not only themselves and clients, but also to the other workers" and "if we're discussing an issue or talking about a piece of work they can throw important light on it from using their experiences" (w).

The inclusion of indigenous workers in the CLASH team was also not without its problems, for example, there was a tendency for workers without such experience to feel marginalised within the project. The employment of indigenous workers, however, should be encouraged. Perhaps ideally the team should consist of workers with a variety of backgrounds and experiences, providing a plurality in approach to the work. But it might also be recommended that sessional or part-time workers in particular, should have an indigenous status. It was not uncommon for clients to express an interest in part-time work, and there is some merit to the suggestion that the recruitment of current prostitutes and drug users greatly facilitates ease of access to current hidden populations (Wiebel, 1988). In employing indigenous workers in this way, it is of course necessary to fully articulate the precise roles the worker is expected to perform, as clearly not all prostitutes and drug users (or 'professional' outreach workers for that matter) make good all-round outreach workers, and each will bring specific areas of expertise to the work.

Evaluating the nature of client contact
As stated above, in order to evaluate the effectiveness of the project in making detached outreach contacts, we also need to consider the nature of clients contacted. Are they from the intended target groups, and are they actually hard-to-reach? Further to this, an assessment can be made regarding clients' relative vulnerability to HIV and other health problems.

In answer to the first of these points, in general terms the project was effective in reaching intended target populations. As reported earlier, where information was known about clients' involvement with prostitution and drug use, almost two-thirds of men contacted were working as rent boys, nearly all (81%) women contacted were working as prostitutes, over a third of clients were injecting drugs, and two-thirds were living in temporary or insecure accommodation. Only 13 clients were known not to be in any of these categories.

There was, however, less overall emphasis on the targeting of drug users by the team than there was with rent boys and women prostitutes. Indeed, while a reasonable proportion of clients contacted were known to be using drugs (28%), a high proportion of them (60%) were also working as prostitutes. There were, for example, no detached outreach sessions which were exclusively oriented towards contacting drug users. There appear to be two reasons for this. First, the emphasis on targeting prostitutes reflected individual workers' interests and expertise within the team, and the team expressed frustration and apprehension about undertaking detached work with drug users. Second, there were other projects working specifically with drug users in central London (e.g.. Hungerford Drug Project, syringe exchanges) but at the time few worked with prostitutes. This enabled CLASH to develop independently of other existing similar projects. However, at the time of writing, there is virtually no regularly scheduled detached outreach work specifically targeting drug users in central London, whereas in contrast there are a number of agencies now working with prostitutes - for example, CLASH, London Connection, Streetwise Youth, Praed Street Working Women's and Men's Projects. In this context, CLASH should re-consider the balance between targeting women prostitutes and rent boys and targeting non-prostitute drug users, placing renewed emphasis on targeting drug users and drug injectors, perhaps in areas other than King's Cross, Victoria and Piccadilly.

It is also worth noting here, that the extent to which particular clients were reached not only varied between but also within intended target populations. Clients working as prostitutes from flats in Soho, for example, were relatively less 'hard-to-reach' than women prostitutes working the streets around King's Cross. This is because they were a 'captive' population and tended to be more organised in terms of their approach to work, money and health. For particular clients, therefore, the CLASH workers realised that quite often those most accessible to contact were also those with most experience of health service contact, and those in less need of the project's services. Although this may have been generally the case, it is nonetheless important to note that the converse was true, and it was not unusual for clients to be in contact with a range of services, sometimes spanning both voluntary and statutory health services, and yet remain in need of particular services or have yet to recognise particular health needs. But as two of the workers commented of women prostitutes contacted in the Soho flats:

"Although the contact was incredibly important and I thought it was very useful in terms of say well-women services, in fact the women that we contacted and the women who had accepted us were the kind of women who were in quite a lot of control anyway... and who were using condoms and insisting on condoms and who had been for quite a long time, and who were actually very aware of HIV and other STDs" (w).

"The women who we contacted who were saying 'no' were probably the women who we really should have been talking with but couldn't" (w).

So although falling within intended target populations, the contacts with women prostitutes working from flats may in general be considered less efficient contacts than those with street working prostitutes from King's Cross. In this respect, it is encouraging to note that nearly two thirds (63%) of new contacts with women prostitutes were with women working in the King's Cross area. It is also encouraging that the numbers of street working and flat working women prostitutes re-contacted are similar, while the number of re-contacts per client contacted in the Soho flats is greater than that in King's Cross (five as opposed to three times). The balance of new contacts and re-contacts achieved with women prostitutes working in Soho and King's Cross therefore appears to reflect their relative need in terms of service contact and service provision.

As far as the contacts made by the team with men working as prostitutes were concerned, there were few with male prostitutes working from agencies, as escorts or as masseurs. In this sense, it is encouraging that CLASH's contacts with rent boys may generally be considered to represent the less organised, more chaotic male prostitutes (Robinson, 1989). But whether as a result they were necessarily 'harder-to-reach' is questionable: accessing escort agencies may be just as difficult as accessing street working rent boys, just as for example, the traditionally hard-to-reach street drug user may actually be 'easier-to-reach' than the more discrete middle class drug user. So, not only did the extent to which clients were 'hard-to-reach' directly influence the extent to which contact was made between intended target populations, it also influenced the extent to which contact can be considered more or less efficient within target populations. The CLASH team were aware of this, and they were careful to target those they considered to be most vulnerable to HIV infection. Having at various points discussed the possibilities of broadening contacting strategies to include for example female and male prostitutes working as escorts, as masseurs and advertising/working from home (which of course, would increase the numbers of contacts made), the team agreed to concentrate on existing target groups since they considered them generally at greater risk of HIV infection and thus in greater need of their services (Fieldnotes, 1989-1990).

As we have said, the CLASH team were conscious of which of their client groups appeared more or less in need of their outreach services, and which were more or less in contact with other agencies and organisations. In the light of CLASH's objectives, one of the most significant indicators of whether or not clients were 'hard-to-reach' was their extent of contact with voluntary and statutory health services. As suggested by a member of the Steering Group:

"The whole point of CLASH is to access people that are not being accessed - either by the Health Service or by other voluntary organisations" (s).

Of the 741 clients contacted by CLASH, 20% were known to be in current contact with other agencies, 21% were known not to be in contact, whilst for the majority (59%) this information was not known. For those where this information was unknown, the likelihood is that they were not in contact with services, particularly statutory based ones. Of those in contact, fewer were in contact with services based in the statutory sector. This can be considered evidence in support of the fact that CLASH's client group were indeed 'hard-to-reach'.

When assessing the quality of the detached outreach contact, therefore, a number of points need to be examined. These include, not only the extent to which target populations were reached, but also clients' vulnerability to HIV, clients' health behaviour, needs for health services, needs for CLASH's services, and the suitability of outreach services provided. These are discussed below.

Facilitating access to services and the problem of referral

As put forward by one of the statutory managers, one of the "principle aims" of CLASH, once contacts had been developed, was to "find access in the health service" for their clients.

In the previous chapter we noted the extent to which clients were referred, where they were referred and the extent to which these referrals were successful. On point of first contact, the CLASH team referred 12% of clients to other agencies, the majority of which were to agencies in the statutory sector. On point of re-contact with clients, CLASH referred 10% of clients, again mostly to statutory agencies. Other than the referral of clients, the team also made specific arrangements for further contact with 13% of clients on first contact, and with 17% of clients on re-contact. The effectiveness of these arrangements are discussed separately later in this chapter.

Perceptions and expectations

As with other CLASH objectives, critical actors had differing views and expectations about the objective of referral. Differing interpretations of the role of referral in the team's outreach objectives, reflected wider differences in expectations about the role of HIV outreach as a whole.

For some statutory managers, the objective of referring clients into statutory services was seen as "justification" for the CLASH outreach project. As explained by one manager:

"I really don't think we'd be putting all the money that we have done into the CLASH team if it was purely to do street outreach work and to provide free condoms and free works to these people. There is a further aim which is actually to get them to have services, which makes it all worth doing" (s).

The emphasis placed on the spread of objectives between the referral of clients and the provision of *in situ* outreach service was viewed slightly differently from one of the voluntary managers, who saw referral:

"as quite low down on the priorities... The streetwork I think actually exists in its own right. It actually goes out there and does something in its own right. If that identifies people that could be referred and would actually accept a referral and make contact with another agency that's a bonus, and might be twenty-five percent of it, but its not the primary reason for doing the work" (v).

And as pointed out later by the same voluntary manager:

"They (BHA) probably find it harder to accept that CLASH is actually working in its own right just by doing the sort of streetwork or the contact work" (v).

But for others, the balance between the objective of client referral and the provision of *in situ* outreach services was less defined, or appeared of equal importance. The CLASH team themselves tended to view contacting clients and providing outreach services as objectives in their own right, but also saw them as steps in a process where referral was the ultimate aim: "The idea of offering services is only like a carrot to then introduce people to other services" (w). This position was perceived to be consistent with Health Authority expectations: "what management want us to do and what we'd like to do is to get people into services that already exist" (w).

Evaluating referral
But while the CLASH workers may have remained consistent in their description and perception of the project as a "referral agency" - like

most managers (at least statutory) sharing a commitment to achieving referral objectives - in practice, the proportion of clients referred were low (12% new clients, 10% re-contacts), and there was considerable disparity between the number of referrals made and the number of positive referral outcomes. Beyond this, an estimate of the proportion of positive referral outcomes to referrals made is extremely difficult to make, and is probably best avoided. However, it is likely to be less than that reported by other similar outreach projects: in Liverpool, of 117 referrals made with women prostitutes over the two year period January 1989 to December 1990, 36 (31%) were definitely taken up (Maryland Centre Quarterly Surveillance Reports, 1989-1990).

There was general agreement between managers and outreach workers as to whether the project had been effective in achieving referral objectives. As summed up by one statutory representative: "there are objectives which haven't been met, which is actually accessing these people into services", and also by a worker: "I don't think our referrals into other services are very good at all, we just don't do it".

In terms of the perception of outreach work as "justified" by achieving referral objectives, it is necessary to regard the project as ineffective. Should referral objectives prove impossible to meet, one statutory representative went so far as to suggest that: "there would be severe questions over whether we'd want to continue the CLASH project" (s). As long as referral was seen as feasible, there at least needed to be evidence of the project "making progress" in order to convince statutory managers "that it's worth pursuing" (s).

The problem of achieving referral objectives was realised by most critical actors, statutory and voluntary alike: "referral is important but it's traumatic" (w). In considering the difficulties encountered by the team with referrals, three related factors seem especially pertinent, all of which are relevant to critical actors' interpretations of the role of outreach work. These are accessibility, flexibility and relevance of statutory health services to hard-to-reach clients' needs; the structural relations between the CLASH project and the Health Authority; and, closely related to the first, the extent to which hard-to-reach clients actually need, or perceive a need for, statutory health services.

Accessibility and relevance of statutory health services
Hard-to-reach clients are notoriously, and in many cases justifiably, suspicious of the relevance and accessibility of statutory health care services. They often require careful persuasion to approach statutory services, and in practice, referrals are often suggested or arranged in

the knowledge that positive referral outcomes are rare. Aware of this, most voluntary and statutory representatives and outreach workers expressed the need for more accessible and flexible health services, indeed that "CLASH would only be as successful in relationship to how accessible services become" (v):

> "There is no doubt that CLASH feel that they could get more people into health services if the health services were more flexible and approachable" (s).

> "I just think that a lot of services (statutory) just can not be adaptable to the needs of our clients... because they are such huge pieces of machinery. And I think a lot of people still have irrational fears about our clients" (w).

> "I think the services have to change before they can become really accessible to, and appropriate for, people like the CLASH client group" (s).

That making effective referrals was considered "important but traumatic" partly explains the differing emphasis placed on the objectives of referral by critical actors. As one statutory representative explained, as long as existing health services were perceived to be inaccessible to hard-to-reach clients, "there's always going to be a need for this kind of detached 'out-there' work". In other words, the balance between particular objectives - between referring clients and providing *in situ* outreach services - will very much depend on the extent to which they are perceived to be realistic and achievable. The degree to which the CLASH team were paternalistic towards their clients in the sense of making decisions on their behalf about the accessibility and relevance of services, and the extent to which CLASH were responding effectively to clients' expressed views is difficult to determine. Nonetheless, it is for reasons of service accessibility that at least one CLASH worker recognised a change in the emphasis placed on referral objectives by the CLASH team:

> "The initial objectives were to just contact people and pass them on to statutory organisations... I think that is one main objective that has really changed... We don't really do that any more - we kind of get stuff for them, keep the client..." (w).

Although still viewing themselves as a "referral agency" in terms of stated objectives, at the level of actually attempting to provide a tangible service to clients, outreach workers directed the service in ways which appeared immediately relevant and obtainable, making moves towards more comprehensive and independent *in situ* service provision. This can be viewed as a 'ground-level' or 'natural' development emerging from within the outreach work itself, despite the fact that to some managers this "was not what it was set up to do". As one of the workers explained:

"I think its very difficult to look at long term aims when your out there trying to achieve something - you're aims and objectives become so much more immediate" (w).

Indeed, whilst in practice it might be recognised that existing health services may be inflexible and inaccessible to many hard-to-reach clients, this is not to suggest that on the level of objectives, referral should be curtailed. This difference between the expectation of objectives and their realisation may be considered just one example of the gulf in experience and understanding existing between the "desk-sitters" and the "very weird creatures" actually doing the outreach work. Instead of remoulding objectives in any particular direction, therefore, the CLASH "experiment" to achieve client referrals into the Health Service remained protected for two reasons. First, because if referral objectives were not being achieved "there would be severe questions over whether we'd want to continue the CLASH project", and second, as voluntary managers indicated:

"Part of CLASH's role was set up from the outset to be the sort of thing that picks up and identifies the gaps in services, or reflects what services can be improved" (v).

"One of the original aims was to look at why people did not use services and... [to] try and negotiate with those services to be more accessible. So it had a campaigning, political aim in that sense" (v).

In this way, it was CLASH's "responsibility to identify what the problems were so that other people could take that up" (s).

The consensus then suggests that should it not be possible to achieve referrals, at least the CLASH team could provide existing services with explanation for this. At this point, however, the second area of difficulty with the objective of referral emerges: the structural relations between the CLASH project and the Health Authority.

Structural relations between CLASH and the Health Authority
Although voluntary managers shared with statutory representatives the view that CLASH should ideally perform an educational role, informing the Authority of the suitability of available services, there were questions about whether the project had the "adequate power base" to be a realistic instrument of change. Voluntary representatives, perhaps sometimes cynically, tended to view the 'educational' process as at once potentially constructive and potentially destructive:

> "The managers should be using it (the CLASH project) as an essential tool. But in some ways... what happens is the opposite, is that managers see what it's throwing out and it becomes more and more a thorn in their side" (v).

If CLASH was to have a campaigning role how effective could it be?:

> "I would expect CLASH to have a campaigning and advocacy role attempting to change services, to make them more relevant to the people who CLASH are targeting, and equally working on the street to try and re-balance the fact that you haven't got a statutory service that we can refer onto..." (v).

> "The clinical services which are controlled by... the Health Authority... have been unwelcoming to their clients... still overwrought and unwilling to make any radical change to make that different. I think they're quite happy to tinker around the edges and say 'come through the back door'" (v).

There is, then, a contradictory relationship between the desire for CLASH to perform an educative role for Health Service and voluntary managers, and the reality of the structural relations between the project and the Health Authority which constrain (some might say intentionally) such innovation in practice:

> "There is still a tension now around how much influence CLASH can exert to actually get real change happening in the Health Authority" (v).

One statutory manager went so far as to question the extent to which the Health Authority actually wanted CLASH to be effective in achieving referral objectives, channelling yet more clients into already stretched services:

"If I'm really cynical, I don't even know to what extent the Health Authority is interested in having more people access it's health services. Practitioners probably are, but I don't know to what extent Health Authority's are. We're already stretched as it is" (s).

The irony of this was that CLASH's apparent lack of success in achieving referral objectives, was precisely the weapon the Health Authority used in their attempts to retain some control of the CLASH project:

"There have been one or two people around in the past who were very good at keeping the lid on things, and not allowing things to change very much - using different techniques for that, like blaming CLASH because they weren't getting enough clients to access health services, they weren't being successful enough, etc., etc." (s).

This merges with the view of a voluntary manager:

"I think Bloomsbury were getting a bit pissed off with the fact that they weren't picking up loads of people. We all sort of said 'that's your fault, that's not CLASH's fault, we've done our bit, we've got the contacts, we're in the flats, we're in the prisons, etc... That's up to Bloomsbury to look at what their politics are and not to give it to CLASH as some sort of fault in their organisation " (v).

Questions about whether the Health Authority wished to allow the CLASH project the capacity to succeed are inextricably linked with issues of management. To make this point, the view of one statutory manager (also quoted in Chapter Four) will suffice:

"As one of the principal objectives of the CLASH team is to access people into the Health Service, one would have thought you would specifically employ people who would have the skills in order to do that. What we did was to specifically employ people who had the skills to do outreach work - and that's what they've done successfully. We didn't employ people with the skills to manipulate and persuade the Health Service to change - and that's simply what they haven't done" (s).

The CLASH workers themselves also felt that the heart of the problem of referral was structural. When actually making a referral, for example, the team felt unable to negotiate an effective mechanism for referral within the Health Service setting:

"We are still viewed as on the periphery of the Health Authority institutional mould... so to negotiate effective referral, for example, with JPH has been very difficult and still is" (w).

"Now we are at the point of actually referring people, Bloomsbury aren't so willing, or haven't organised good referral procedures to accept clients" (w).

Attempts were made to secure better referral mechanisms, particularly at JPH. One statutory manager felt "they've had a lot of help and they haven't always helped themselves", while one member of the Management Group recognised that many projects in Bloomsbury wanted priority for their clients, and that this was difficult to arrange with the result that even when systems had been established, they would occasionally fail the client. Attempts by the CLASH team to establish a coupon system which allowed clients immediate appointments with "empathetic doctors" at JPH failed in practice as a result of a variety of ostensibly pragmatic reasons. For example, simply because "there was somebody else on the desk who we didn't expect to have on the desk...they'd forgotten, that kind of silly nonsense" (s), because of "receptionists not really knowing who we are" (w), and "because we don't refer often enough to keep ourselves on the map" (w).
In some situations referral arrangements had been "reduced to individual relationships with doctors" (w), and "the numbers of places that we can confidently refer to is still quite small" (w). Thus, referral was viewed as a precarious procedure by the CLASH team. For this reason, there seemed a tendency for the CLASH team to act paternalistically towards, and on behalf of clients. As it was, "a lot of our client group have had very bad experiences with Bloomsbury Health Authority" (w). If clients should have a negative experience on contact with services having been referred by CLASH, the team felt this would alienate them further,

undermining the credibility of the CLASH team among other clients. This in turn could prevent CLASH from making referrals where there was a perceived danger of this happening. As one worker put it: "it will take a lot of time and effort from working with them to establish enough trust before they will even consider accessing a service", and "a singular fuck-up for a client will be devastating - it will have a snowball knock-on effect for the rest of our client group" (w).

So given the pre-existing instability of referrals among hard-to-reach clients and the introduction of referral mechanisms which were precarious in themselves, the outreach workers often felt the Health Authority had failed them and their clients. On this point, they felt confident that voluntary participants agreed:

> "I think that if we said to the voluntary sector - well, three years into CLASH we couldn't refer women to [BHA hospital] for termination because they were HIV positive, which is the situation we're only now trying to address, they would have been shocked by the slowness of it all" (w).

> "I think the voluntary sector are justifiably pissed off with the Health Authority, because two years on there aren't all that many services up and running" (w)

In order to facilitate the ease with which referrals could be made, therefore, the team felt there was a precedent for "management to step in" to negotiate with potential referral services:

> "The reality is that CLASH as we stand can not get the kind of services we need by going round and talking to people. We're not going to be respected because we're not medical people... Half of Bloomsbury doesn't even know who we are... There needs to be a PR thing done - an acceptance of who we are and an understanding" (w).

The team thus felt there was a need for evidence of greater commitment from BHA to accepting and providing services for their clients: the need for "recognition within the statutory sector that we are a statutory organisation which would cut half the crap of referring people out" (w). Conversely, from the Health Service perspective, the willingness to provide such commitment was probably influenced by their need for greater evidence of the project's effectiveness and for evidence of 'visible returns' (see above, this chapter).

That the CLASH team viewed the problem of referral as structural (as did some managers) explains their commitment over time to developing a more *in situ* service: this they saw as a tangible and realistic service to clients. If referral objectives were in practice relatively unattainable, despite in theory a commitment, the services provided to clients must compensate accordingly. This is not to suggest that the objective of referral is *necessarily* unachievable, but that it may in future be considered a secondary outcome of outreach work. Given increasing commitment to accessing and providing services to CLASH's client groups from the Health Service - such as the development of special clinic programmes for CLASH's clients at JPH - and the potential for further commitment to CLASH's referral objectives - such as Health Service managers liaising within the Authority for increased flexibility and accessibility of services - there remains potential for clients to be effectively referred. These points aside, it was the view of one voluntary manager that:

> "It doesn't matter how good a service is, how good the referral you make is, less than fifty percent of the people you refer actually get there anyway" (v).

If CLASH were able to facilitate referrals for those who required them, while also developing appropriate service provision elsewhere, and if such referrals had a fifty percent success rate, most workers and managers involved would surely view this as effective. But before one concludes that referral objectives (as they stand) have yet to be achieved by the CLASH team, the objective itself must be questioned.

Clients' needs for statutory health services
The objective of referral necessarily assumes there is a need and a wish for health services among the hard-to-reach. As we have said, the role of outreach work, for some statutory managers, progresses no further than the principal aim of referral. The third factor relevant to understanding the applicability of referral objectives then, which is also closely related to the accessibility of statutory services to hard-to-reach clients, is the relevance of the objective itself: to what extent did clients have or perceive a need for the services and health care on offer.

Participant observations in street detached settings with rent boys in Victoria, Piccadilly and Euston have confirmed that outreach contacts often remain as understated as possible so as not to draw the attention of police, punters or pimps, and usually are brief, sometimes hasty interventions. Even when more lengthy and relaxed contacts (perhaps ten minutes or so) were possible, gaining a clear understanding of clients' health needs beyond their more pressing concerns about housing, accommodation, money and so on remained difficult. In this context, unless clients were able to recognise and vocalise their needs for primary care services, assessment of their needs in practice was a time-consuming business, and was more likely to occur on subsequent re-contacts with clients. As one of the outreach workers outlined, the possibilities for referral were not only restricted by inadequate referral procedures or inflexible services, but also by the brevity and restrictions of the street outreach contact:

"I don't think we're getting as many people into services as we should be because we don't have enough time to go through things on the street" (w).

In practice, it proved quite incorrect to merely presume that most hard-to-reach clients had a need - or were able to recognise a need - for health services. As CLASH workers mentioned, some of their clients, particularly women prostitutes working from flats in Soho, "were in quite a lot of control anyway" and "a lot of them already have services elsewhere" (w). Participant observations of a mobile unit run by the Working Men's Project at St. Mary's which collaborated with CLASH while being piloted, provide further backing to these comments. Although the unit was positioned in Soho and Victoria, ready to give STD and medical checks for rent boys referred through outreach work, it was nearly impossible to refer rent boys in practice. This was as much a problem about articulating what was on offer - in the face of there being little interest in things beyond food, money and shelter - as it was a problem about the practicalities of actually encouraging a contact to get there had they recognised the need (which in practice only few did).

So, the objectives of referral may be more appropriate for some target groups than for others. But here too is a problem. It is precisely the clients who are more likely to need a referral service (for example, women working King's Cross as opposed to Soho flats) who are also more unlikely to recognise the need (and who are also probably 'harder-to-reach'). In cases where the outreach worker was simply presented with 'bigger' and more immediate client problems than issues of referral (which was by far the majority of cases), the extent to which outreach workers felt able to promote effective HIV health education and to recognise clients' medical service requirements over and above emotional, social and welfare needs were slim:

> "It's quite heart aching when you're contacting people who need housing, who need to get their DHSS money. And you know that at the end of the day there isn't anything you can do for them practically..." (w).

There may be the tendency then, for the objectives of referral - if not partly of outreach - to assume that what hard-to-reach populations require is precisely that which they have so systematically and effectively avoided: in this case - statutory health services. Beyond this, the services which hard-to-reach clients are most likely to identify a need for appear to be social rather than medical. There is perhaps a danger of overlooking reasons why populations are hard-to-reach in the first place, and why they have had good reason to avoid certain types of service delivery. These and related points of discussion are considered in the concluding chapter.

Supply and demand: Service delivery and service need

CLASH was set up with the dual purpose of providing an *in situ* street health education service and referral access into appropriate general health care and HIV-specific statutory and voluntary services. We have considered the efficiency with which CLASH were able to access their clients into health services, and below we discuss the balance between these complementary services under issues of service development. Here we will consider the extent to which CLASH's *in situ* service provision reflected the project's original objectives to provide preventive materials and health advice, and the extent to which it can be considered an effective means of preventing HIV infection.

The main street based services provided to clients were condoms, injecting equipment, leaflets, project cards (including other local drug and HIV projects), spermicide and lubricants. As one of the workers said, "we're quite good at offering the practical tools of the trade"(w). In fact, in the vast majority of contacts, women prostitutes (92%) and rent boys (73%) were provided with condoms, and drug injectors with clean injecting equipment (75%). Furthermore, the regularity with which women prostitutes, particularly those working from Soho flats, passed through the CLASH office to collect condoms and injecting equipment steadily increased throughout the evaluation period (Fieldnotes, 1990). There was probably little doubt between workers and managers that the CLASH team were distributing a great deal of preventive equipment, especially condoms, among their intended target populations.[1]

Indeed, this members of the Steering Group acknowledged, but some felt there was rather more to know:

> "They are getting condoms to them and so on, but they have somehow been reluctant to give a very clear sense of what their work involved, and what they were doing... I think there is probably too much defensiveness about what's going on, too much over protection of clients" (s).

> "CLASH don't talk too much about the detail of their streetwork" (s).

In fact, what these members of Steering Group wished to know, was precisely how effective CLASH were being on the street: what else were CLASH doing apart from distributing free condoms, and to what effect? From the Health Service perspective, it was essential to know precisely what CLASH were doing, as evidence of the project's effectiveness was required in order to plan and manage outreach services systematically. The question of project effectiveness can be considered in stages: to what extent did clients want or require anything apart from condoms? To what extent were CLASH actually able to do anything beyond distributing condoms? And consequently, how effective were the outreach contacts in actually encouraging clients' attempts to prevent HIV?

In response to the first two of these points, it would be short-sighted to view CLASH as nothing more than a mobile chemist or a condom delivery service. As we indicated above, CLASH's client group brought to the project's outreach work a diversity of service needs. Some were more able to recognise and vocalise their needs than others. Similarly, the CLASH team were able to contact some clients more efficiently than others (i.e. the 'greater' the client need, the more 'efficient' the contact). A selection of clients, it is fair to say, did not perceive or express a need, and sometimes did not have a need, for services beyond the supply of condoms:

> "We gave them free condoms, but I think they were using condoms anyway. So I'm not sure what we did in terms of HIV

prevention. I mean, we might have done things in terms of making the face of the Health Authority more accessible" (w).

But for most other clients, who were unable or unwilling to buy condoms or injecting equipment, the CLASH service - simply on the level of distribution - was a welcome one. As a recent extract from the evaluator's fieldnotes of outreach work in Victoria demonstrates:

> "He rather reluctantly took a packet of HT's, took one condom out of the box and gave the rest back to me. (This was the same as the other week). But I was surprised by his response when I mentioned carrying needles. We didn't know he was injecting, but he was pleased to take some, though at the same time careful not to let his friends see..." (Fieldnotes, 1991).

It is clear then that the CLASH team were effective in providing preventive materials to their clients. On most of the outreach contacts we observed, the outreach worker when describing the CLASH service would offer at least condoms, if not also injecting equipment, and would go on to outline the advice and opportunities the project was able to offer should clients be concerned about a particular health issue or wish to see a doctor or counsellor. Of course, as outreach workers were aware (much to their own frustration) it was "impossible to measure", "impossible to judge" whether simply distributing condoms would result in the reduction of HIV related harm for their clients (w). Rather, they were doing all they felt they could do, offering more than just condoms, in the hope they could encourage clients to recognise their health needs (should they actually have any) and utilise the variety of services on offer. In this respect, the team often tended to define the effectiveness of contacts in terms of the extent to which clients appreciated the availability of such a service, whether or not they were in need of it:

> "It's a case of 'do you need this or do you need that', they appreciate that. Some people don't because they are so used to that way of life that they can't accept anything other" (w).

The CLASH team's perceived ability to make the outreach contact 'work' in the clients' favour brings us to the specific question of how efficient is the outreach contact itself in providing and realising opportunities for client's health and service needs. This is as much a question about the nature of outreach work, as it is a question about the effectiveness of the CLASH team.

On the majority of outreach contacts there was little opportunity for constructive discussion about clients' vulnerability to health problems: "on the street you have such limited time that you really can't go into it all" (w); "you don't need to get into conversation, not on initial contact" (w). This point was also noted when on outreach observations in Victoria:

> "There is only time to ask whether condoms, works and cards are wanted, give them out, and say perhaps a sentence or two about being able to provide access to other health services for clients, and this generally speaking is the extent of the street contact" (Fieldnotes, 1990).

Under these circumstances, and with clients often being unable to recognise specific health problems over and above their more pressing basic problems about housing or finance, the team often felt powerless to do anything more than lend immediate advice or "send them to a place that might be able to help" (w). As commented by one voluntary manager:

> "CLASH in itself was never going to be a practical service in that sense. It was the first contact on the street, and then people could be referred into those agencies which were going to meet their needs" (v).

The street contacts which seemed to provide most opportunity for depth client work, were those in which clients were referred on for further direction or help, or those in which clients were encouraged to come to CLASH's own drop-in service. As illustrated by a recent extract from the evaluator's observation fieldnotes:

> "While [name of co-worker] dealt with [client name] I sat with my back to them both talking with [female client name] and three of her friends. I'd seen her at least three times before (she also knew me by sight), and this was the first opportunity I'd had to actually speak with her. I knew [male name] worked and had given him condoms before, but hadn't known that [female client name] was his girlfriend... once I told [female client name] about the Friday clinic she said she was 'in need of a doctor' saying 'the

doctors around here are no good'. I assured her we had female doctors who were really nice and that she should come up one Friday. She said she wanted to and would try to come... I hope she does, but if she doesn't, I still felt this was a good contact. At last we managed to contact her having seen her on the periphery of the scene for sometime" (Fieldnotes, 1991).

However, as we know from the discussion above, 'successful' client referrals were few. In contrast, the rate with which CLASH were able to encourage clients to the office premises was slightly more favourable, although still slow. For specific health problems or client issues, however, the team successfully re-contacted clients on 75% of the occasions where they had made specific arrangements for further contact. Even so, the extent to which the outreach contact effectively provided opportunities for the realisation of, and provision for, clients' health needs remains extremely difficult to determine. Clearly, the outreach contact can be considered 'effective' in all cases on the level of having once reached appropriate target groups it is at least able to offer a variety of services, the minimum of which is the distribution of preventive materials, so allowing clients the means and opportunity to prevent the spread of HIV infection. Beyond this, their relative efficacy is variable and the chances for extended service delivery with clients slim: re-contacts were in a small minority; new contacts were brief and restricted; clients were often unable to recognise specific health needs; clients often had no need or wish to be referred to statutory or any other services; positive referral outcomes were tiny in number; and the chances of discussing clients' HIV health needs in depth usually minimal.

Furthermore, as detailed in Chapter Six, there were no strong indicators of change in clients' HIV and health behaviour throughout the monitoring period. Given the small number of changes which occurred, it is impossible to suggest whether or not they occurred as a result of, or under influence from, the CLASH intervention. Rather than highlighting the lack of proof for the effectiveness of HIV outreach work, this quite forcefully demonstrates the practical problems involved in evaluating outreach intervention. For example, the problems of gaining reliable data over time to measure change were compounded not only by the fact that the amount of information known or possible to collect in outreach settings was limited, but by the fact that the proportion of clients re-contacted over any reasonable length of time was minimal, and that different outreach workers re-contacting the same client 'knew' different information from one another.

In this context, the value of the HIV outreach contact can continue to be seen as an effective way to deliver and educate about preventive materials such as condoms and injecting equipment, as well as providing the potential for catering for hard-to-reach clients' primary care, medical and other health needs. This latter function might be further encouraged should a number of the problems mentioned above be alleviated. Suggestions for improvement might include broadening the range of services on offer to cater for clients' immediate and most pressing problems of housing and finance, improving the possibilities for more lengthy and detailed communication in street and community based settings (see below), and relying less on existing primary care and medical services, instead providing them directly in the community (see below).

Cost effectiveness

One final question which must be addressed when evaluating the effectiveness of the outreach contact is cost effectiveness. The outreach contact is a costly way to contact clients, particularly (and perhaps increasingly) from a Health Service perspective. A crude estimate from CLASH's extent of contact will suffice to demonstrate: a total of 741 clients and a total of 1383 separate contacts averaging approximately ten minutes each were made by approximately four workers in approximately 2400 days of total project time allocated to detached outreach work, which meant it took an average of 3.2 days for the project to contact each new client, and an average of 1.7 days for the project to make each outreach contact. Although detailed actual costings were unavailable, in terms of approximate allocated staffing costs throughout the evaluation period (total of £222,993.00, costed at 1991 staffing levels of £86,320 per year) this gives a cost of £300.93 per every new contact and a cost of £161.24 per each outreach contact. Of course, these estimates are based on time and money allocated rather than invested, and such wildly approximate estimations can do more damage than good, and are often meaningless when presented alone without explanation or context (see above and Chapter Six in this respect). But the point here, is that it is a question of the criteria by which the outreach contact is to be evaluated that is of importance, not necessarily the figures in themselves.

In general terms, the 'problem of outreach work' when compared with other forms of service delivery is that the costs of input relative to output are extremely high, especially when expecting immediate or visible returns. This, quite simply, may be inherent in outreach work. This is not to suggest that the efficiency and quality of the outreach contact and service delivery is beyond improvement (otherwise there would be little point in evaluation), but rather to emphasise the importance of providing realistic and practical criteria for the practice of making judgements about the effectiveness of a particular intervention.

It therefore may be pointlessly regressive to simply criticise outreach as inefficient purely on the basis of its cost per contact when compared to other more conventional interventions. A realistic assessment of 'cost-effectiveness' must somehow judge the relative value of reaching a comparatively small group of people, which are often incredibly hard-to-reach, in order to provide them with opportunities in which they may or may not take interest. This may be a difficult question, especially for a Health Authority unsure of the extent to which the outreach contact provides real opportunities for catering for clients' health needs and unconvinced by the relevance and value of referral objectives. But this logic may also be misleading. First, because the practicalities of outreach work often make the use of formal and systematic evaluation methods problematic (see Chapter Two). To borrow the words of a statutory manager, the practicalities are:

> "that you can't always demonstrate the effectiveness of things that you do, which is not a reason for not doing them. That's not very managerial but it's true" (s).

Second, it may be precisely because hard-to-reach populations have been viewed and defined as such that they in fact remain hard-to-reach. As the above statutory manager also remarked:

> "I have a gut feeling that whatever it costs, doing what they [CLASH] are doing would not happen unless they did it" (s).

Rather than questioning the relative cost of reaching the hard-to-reach on criteria the same or similar for assessing more conventional health programmes, the cost effectiveness of outreach must be considered on its own terms. Put simply, if Health Authority's are genuinely committed to reaching the hard-to-reach, then in theory they should also commit themselves to providing the necessary resources to reach them, include them and cater for their needs. If in trying to do this, it is discovered that there is little interest in the services which they have to offer (which may not be a surprise given hard-to-reach clients' avoidance of them), then this is not necessarily a time to question the cost effectiveness of reaching and providing for the hard-to-reach, but rather a time for planning and developing alternative and complementary services.

Suggesting that the cost effectiveness of outreach programmes should be evaluated on their own terms and criteria, is not to suggest that interventions should be encouraged simply as inherently cost effective. Outreach interventions can indeed be seen as warranted in that they aim to provide services where there is little or no such provision. As long as there is a *need* for such provision - whether it be located alongside existing services or independently in the community - and as long as the clients' remain hard-to-reach in the sense of having little or no contact with services, and if indeed this can be demonstrated, in broad humanitarian terms this can be considered cost effective. But this view does not detract from the concomitant need to systematically evaluate cost effectiveness. Regular feedback on project effectiveness is necessary in order to plan and develop services according to clients' needs. Furthermore, as suggested above, if in the event of systematic evaluation there is little or no evidence of effectiveness or of 'visible returns', then this may be a time for re-directing the nature and focus of service delivery. For instance, on the basis of findings which show the achievement of referral objectives to be unlikely, there is a need to re-evaluate the relative cost effectiveness and priority of pursuing this particular objective. In this particular example, greater efficiency and greater cost effectiveness might be achieved if referral into existing services is considered a secondary objective for those clients who identify such a need, while the increased adoption of *in situ* primary health services may cater for those unable or unwilling to be referred into existing services.

In order to evaluate the cost effectiveness and efficiency of particular project objectives, evaluation must be considered an essential and integral component of service delivery. Perhaps of most importance is the evaluation of clients' expressed needs for, and perceptions of, a project's appropriateness and effectiveness. Without involving clients directly in evaluation, it becomes difficult to determine the effectiveness of service delivery. Indeed, the CLASH team had ultimate control over the flow of information regarding clients' views about the project, and in the context of management conflict, it is difficult to determine to what extent clients' needs were assumed by project workers (for example, regarding needs for statutory health services) and protected from management rather than negotiated with both clients and managers.

Certainly, many members of the Steering Group felt there was a need for greater evidence of project effectiveness with regard to clients' perceptions of the service. It may therefore be considered unfortunate that an independent evaluation of this kind was denied access to clients and thus also of their opinions. The efficiency with which we manage and develop our outreach service responses must be carefully and systematically monitored and evaluated in order to facilitate the necessary and practical steps towards improving the distribution of outreach resources and towards improving the health choices of the hard-to-reach. It is fundamental that this process should involve hard-to-reach clients themselves.

Service development: Basic issues and the way forward

Impetus to develop the outreach services offered by CLASH in any particular direction, as we have seen above, were influenced by individuals' perceptions of which of the objectives were achievable. In evaluating the extent to which proposals for service development were in accordance with the project's stated objectives, the following two points will be considered: the nature and merit of the team's proposals for service development; and the differences between individuals' views and expectations of service development.

Largely as a result of finding referral unsuccessful the CLASH team felt a need to develop and expand services in ways which they saw as more realistic to client needs. This involved attempting to accommodate more primary care services directly in the community, either within the existing team or at least outside of existing Health Service structures, rather than make further attempts to develop links with existing services:

> "I would like to see the project have a lot more workers and be doing a lot more work... We should have someone with medical professional skills within our team" (w).

The team's attempts to move in this direction were most clearly expounded in their proposals for a mobile outreach unit and for a women's drop-in and health centre to be situated within easy access from King's Cross. The outreach workers felt that this would facilitate the recognition of clients' needs for primary care services as well as encouraging accessibility and flexibility of service provision:

"What we're saying by the mobile unit and the women's centre is that people are not getting the services they want and therefore there needs to be something else" (w).

As we discussed above, the team felt the reasons for clients "not getting the services they want" were not only a result of inadequate referral procedures and inapplicable services on offer, but also because the street outreach contact was restricted, allowing little room for in-depth discussion about particular health issues or problems. In contrast, bringing the services into the community would allow possibilities for immediate referral to services accessible and available and developed according to clients' expressed needs.

The worker who was responsible for preparing the proposal for the mobile outreach unit said of the two proposals:

"The basic bottom line is that CLASH have said 'at the end of the day we can't bring people into services as much as you want'. The way of doing this is to bring the services out to them, to have a clinic that's open in the evening for women working as prostitutes because those women would go to a clinic at half past nine at night, but they wouldn't go at half nine in the morning. Clients will not come into JPH for a check-up but they might if doctors went out in a van and talked about the services they can get, and the doctors could say 'I'll be in the clinic tomorrow, you know me now, why don't you come along'. Clients may not want to come along to the needle exchange, but they would be happy to get clean works from a mobile unit..." (w).

But there was a difference in emphasis among workers as to the nature of the services to be provided by the unit. As another worker suggests, the above worker "mistook it...to have all these kinds of people in the back of a van. And that's not the idea. The idea is to physically get the workers to another place..." and:

"The mobile unit is basically because with the police presence people are being scattered and moved on... I know that when we go down to King's Cross we're going to see women, but I also know that a lot of them have gone up to Stamford Hill. We can't do Stamford Hill and King's Cross" (w).

The use of a mobile outreach unit as a method to provide increased mobility to outreach locations or to provide more comprehensive outreach health services *have* been effectively implemented elsewhere. The best established of these is the outreach methadone bus in Amsterdam, which combines both of these complementary aims (Buning *et al.*, 1988). Methadone is seen as an integral feature of Amsterdam's Municipal Health Service harm minimisation programme. The methadone buses have been in operation since 1979, and provide methadone prescriptions, a syringe exchange facility, condoms, information and advice and a general health service. The intervention, therefore, provides low threshold on-site access to general primary health care services, as well as HIV-specific ones. Similar mobile outreach services have been established to positive effect elsewhere in New Jersey (Jackson *et al.*, 1987), and New York (Reid, 1989), and in the UK in Liverpool (Newcombe, 1989) and Plymouth (Roberts, 1989).

The idea of establishing community drop-in centres with the aim of providing for clients contacted through outreach work is less common. In Birmingham, the Safe Project established a drop-in and clinic for women prostitutes contacted through outreach work in late 1989 (Safe Project, 1990). The clinic offers family planning, genito-urinary, cervical cytology and HIV counselling services. As yet there is no available monitoring or evaluation data.

Perhaps the best established drop-in and health centre is the Mobile Prostitute Contact Centre in Utrecht. Working on similar principles to CLASH's proposed centre, the centre was opened in 1986, with the aim of providing both drop-in facilities as well as opportunities for primary care and medical check-ups with doctors. Situated in the prostitution area of Utrecht, the centre has proved popular and effective. Since 1986, over 60,000 condoms have been distributed, and throughout 1987, 180 prostitutes visited the centre, with an average of 20 visits each night (Buning, 1990).

The immediate response from the Steering Group to the team's proposals for developing their outreach services was a request for clarification, although some managers were immediately negative. This was the response of one statutory manager:

"They're asking for things now like drop-in centres, like a mobile bus. Now there's absolutely no doubt that the project could not operate the present outreach services they're doing plus a mobile bus, plus a mobile centre... They can't do everything - an outreach team is not a drop-in centre" (s).

For most voluntary managers, however, these proposals were seen as a "natural development of CLASH", as "just a more sophisticated form of outreach" (v). As one voluntary manager explained:

"If it's seen as coming out of the work with the client group that is what is important - so long as the service is a needs-related service" (v).

The main problem for statutory managers was that the proposals seemed to conflict with the team's stated aims and objectives, particularly of referral:

"Is it one of their aims and objectives to provide drop-in services or is it to access them [clients] into other services? And I actually think that CLASH are thinking differently to everybody else on that... I'm still holding onto this original thing which was the idea to access into other services" (s).

Indeed, the CLASH team probably were "thinking differently to everybody else" (and also on occasions to each other), viewing the proposals for the mobile unit and women's health centre as a natural development of their service provision. As a result of the Steering Group's response, the team felt that they had not "really had the financial back-up to open our services", becoming tired of "basically putting those items on the agenda again and again" and feeling they had been "rather set up for failure, because we've tried to develop services for our client group and there isn't the money to pay for it" (w).

The difference in the thinking of the CLASH team to that of their managers (particularly statutory managers) regarding project service development appears to be rooted in wider differences in approach and service provision as a whole. The foundation for CLASH's response was based on their experiences of attempting to provide outreach services to clients. As one of the team was aware: "we're working CLASH round the clients rather than the clients round us". In contrast, their managers - particularly statutory ones - viewed service development from the point of view of being service providers. For example, as one statutory representative remarked "you don't develop a service that people can access simply because you want to do something with these people".

This difference in opinion, appears to reflect wider tensions in the conceptualisation of health between bottom-up negotiated approaches and top-down prescriptive approaches. The tensions experienced in practice were precisely those which the CLASH integrated model of outreach attempted to go some way towards confronting by collaboration between voluntary and 'community' representatives with those from a 'professional' and top-down perspective.

The real problem with these proposals, as one of the statutory managers remarked, was not so much that they conflicted with the achievement of specific project objectives (like referral), but that moves towards a more comprehensive independent outreach service provision were "changing the nature of what we mean by services": the difference is "ideological" (s). In other words, these service developments challenged the ways in which service delivery should be organised: "the street has a right to be there and has a right to have services provided for it" (s).

In practice these tensions had to be resolved. According to one statutory manager, CLASH had to "turn the ideological into something that the statutory will understand":

> "It's no good coming to a meeting and saying you'd like to have a mobile unit. You've got to present it like an advertising package because of the world we're living in now. You don't like it, but if you want to get on - you know, if you want to work on the streets you've got to make those compromises" (s).

This quote once again refers to the "managerial cultural differences" operating between outreach workers and statutory managers; indicating the Health Authority's need for evidence of project effectiveness and project accountability on the one hand, and the project's desire to develop services in response to clients' needs on the other. As suggested earlier, the conflicts which ensued over the CLASH project's recommendations for service delivery were inextricably linked with the conflicts occurring throughout the management process (see Chapter Four and Five). Without the management skills required "to turn the ideological into something the statutory will understand", the team had little chance of effecting the necessary and appropriate changes in the direction of their outreach services. But just as the differences in management stemmed from competing ideological positions, so did the differences in perception and expectation about the role and objectives of outreach work. In this respect, whether or not CLASH were able to present their ideas in the form of "an advertising package", the same deep-seated conflicts may have emerged.

These tensions over the nature of the project's service development raise important considerations about the assumptions embedded in the

CLASH model of outreach as a whole. They also have direct implications for the design and implementation of similar models of outreach service delivery and management in the future.

CHAPTER EIGHT

INNOVATION AND CONSTRAINT: IMPLICATIONS FOR POLICY AND PRACTICE

In the urgency to provide immediate responses to ameliorate the further spread of HIV infection among hard-to-reach populations, there has been a tendency to search for 'innovative', if not idealistic models of service delivery. In the process, 'outreach' has become a fast expanding field. In general terms, this has facilitated an encouraging departure from information-giving and individualistic modes of health education. More specifically, and running parallel with this, there has been an increased tendency to view outreach itself as an innovative creation, open to ownership and utilisation from all service quarters.

It is encouraging that outreach should increasingly be the concern of both voluntary and statutory health service sectors. This is especially the case if such commitments are pursued in the interests of collaboration, rather than competition, with the aim of integrated service provision, rather than a confused collection of separate service identities. The CLASH project seemed just such a creation. It combined voluntary and statutory health sector interest, it integrated voluntary and statutory sector service provision, and it was jointly managed between the two sectors. This was precisely why it was considered so innovative. This 'innovation' is encouraging, but one must assess critically precisely what it means in practice. Would statutory services have woken up to the idea of providing for the hard-to-reach had it not been for HIV? What does this tell us about the nature and terms of the collaboration? What exactly is 'innovative' about such intersectoral collaboration? To what extent do they actually encourage innovation in practice?

Outreach health education, though historically grounded in a variety of service perspectives including youth and community work, philanthropy, social and political reform, self help, research and ethnography, and public health (Rhodes *et al.*, 1991a), remains closest to the principles and practices of bottom-up community-based intervention. With the growing interest in intersectoral collaboration over community health, 'external' (e.g. NHS initiated) and 'internal' (generated within communities themselves) approaches to community intervention have increasingly begun to share the same aims and objectives. These include those objectives, previously the concern of 'internal' initiatives, of redressing health inequalities, providing for communities marginalised by conventional health service responses, and involving them in the process of education, prevention and change.

What may sometimes be considered 'innovative' about these collaborative approaches, however, is less that they aim specifically to achieve these objectives, particularly the broader aims of facilitating collective or social change directly in the community, but that they *are* collaborations. So by definition it is 'innovative' that established health services should attempt to provide for the previously marginalised, but not so for those community based responses which have had a long commitment in this area. It is therefore of crucial importance not only to question *what* it is which is 'innovative', but *how* innovative these collaborations will prove to be. For it is almost inevitable that intersectoral collaborations of this type bring with them (as did the CLASH intervention) many opposing and competing viewpoints from the divergent theoretical positions involved. And this union of 'differences', although 'innovative' in principle and structure, may result in innovation being constrained when it comes to practice. It has not been unusual, for example, for past attempts by statutory health, local and central governments to provide 'liberal' responses to service provision to have resulted in the dilution of 'innovative' responses (or at least the dilution of truly community-based responses) in practice. The disbanding of the HEA's Professional and Community Development Division is but one example (Webster, 1991), the Government's disapproval of the term 'community development for health' for carrying echoes of a social philosophy thought to be outdated is one other (Beattie, 1991), and the conflicts experienced in the organisation and practice of recent 'innovative' service responses like HIV outreach intervention (and CLASH) may be a third. With the advent of HIV infection and AIDS, and at a time when collaboration may be both more feasible and more likely than before, it is timely that these important issues are addressed with both speed and a critical perspective.

The findings presented from this evaluation show the CLASH project to be have been characterised at once by innovation and constraint. There was, and clearly remains, an urgent need to provide tangible and realistic opportunities of service provision for the hard-to-reach and those without equal access to general health care and HIV specific services. In this sense there remains a need to provide a comprehensive and integrated network of service provision in an attempt to 'bridge' gaps between existing, if often disparate, service responses. This necessitates an element of collaboration between those with experience and expertise in providing community-based intervention and those without such experience and expertise but with a range of services on offer.

The findings presented in the previous chapters show the potential for conflict in collaborations of this type. These conflicts and tensions were paradoxically precisely those which the collaboration attempted to acknowledge and exploit to its advantage. The essential problem with the CLASH intervention was that the union of 'differences' in styles of management and service delivery, rather than becoming the source for mutual learning, compromise and adjustment, often became further entrenched purely as differences. This is not to say that the three critical actors involved (CLASH, the voluntary sector and the Health Authority) had no urge to collaborate, but rather that a combination of problems in the functioning of management structure and circumstance rendered the practice of collaboration problematic. Many of the conflicts which ensued were probably expected, as each of the participants brought to the collaboration a range of competing viewpoints about health education practice and service delivery. But the problem was that the collaboration, slow to 'learn' how to collaborate, was never able to move constructively beyond the point of initial conflict and misunderstanding. In the context of the CLASH project colluding with many of the voluntary participants and competing with the Health Authority, the Steering Group (the interface for collaboration) became the battleground for conflict. The Health Authority would retrench into the practice of authoritative sanctioning and the voluntary sector would attack statutory managers as inflexible, over-bureaucratic and unresponsive. The 'differences' between participants in the collaboration became the terms by which the problems of management were articulated, and contributed to the essence of the conflict itself: it was not simply that participants *would* not collaborate, circumstances (mainly the increasing unmanageability of the CLASH team) often meant they *could* not.

In this context it is difficult to determine to what extent the Health Authority became inflexible and controlling as a result of pre-existing conflict in the management process rather than as a result of being institutionally incapable of managing an outreach project both efficiently and effectively. Nonetheless, if outreach is to become an effective HIV prevention strategy, then the nature of its service delivery and development must remain clearly rooted in a 'community' perspective. Fundamental to this perspective, is the negotiation and participation with clients in the process of education and prevention, and the facilitation, if possible, of collective and community change. This necessarily involves the clients in the planning and organisation of service developments; a process of empowerment rather than paternalism or prescription, where clients' needs are neither assumed or prescribed. In this way, outreach has the capacity to challenge dominant modes of health education (of which Health Authority's are often a part) which are often characterised by authoritarian, prescriptive and paternalistic approaches restricting change to the individual. In the context of HIV prevention, and as statutory and existing health services attempt to adapt to cater for the hard-to-reach, there may be a danger of losing sight of the fundamental value of what outreach and community-based prevention responses have to offer. On the one hand there may be a danger of institutionalisation and on the other of prescription: both of which cannot meet the axiomatic principles of outreach to provide a client responsive service on clients' terms.

As we have seen in previous chapters, the Health Authority indeed did become authoritative and prescriptive as to the development of the CLASH project's outreach services. While, for example, the CLASH workers attempted to develop services in ways they saw as immediately tangible and realistic for their clients, by proposing greater community based and *in situ* service provision, many statutory managers preferred the project to remain loyal to its "primary aim" of referral; the "justification" for its outreach work. This particular conflict (between referring into statutory services and providing alternative community based services) highlights the extreme opposites of the collaboration: whereas the Health Authority wished to provide services for the hard-to-reach within an existing and pre-defined framework of service provision, the CLASH workers and voluntary participants felt it more appropriate to develop services responsive to need, outside of the existing services on offer.

Here then, may be a fundamental difference between participants as to the role and definition of outreach work. On the one hand, the approach is 'top-down', attempting to institutionalise (trying to fit existing services into hard-to-reach clients' needs), and on the other, the approach is 'bottom-up', attempting to de-institutionalise, to provide what clients' say they need. Of course in practice, these differences were often more confused and less polarised, and there is a problem in determining precisely the extent to which the CLASH team's attempts to provide services according to clients' needs were also an attempt simply to subvert existing service responses. There was the possibility, for example, that the appearance of differences were accentuated by the CLASH team's overly paternalistic approach to clients, and needs were sometimes assumed (rather than negotiated) to be better catered for outside existing statutory service provision. Furthermore, from the

Health Authority's perspective, in order to plan and develop the alternative and improved services suggested by the CLASH team, there was a need for 'visible returns', for *evidence* of client need. With little such evidence, largely because the evaluation was unable to gain direct access to clients to investigate such matters, such recommendations were viewed by many statutory managers with caution as to their motivations and origins.

These conflicts emerged too in the management of CLASH. Rather like the historical development of syringe exchange, at the level of management functioning the CLASH project has become institutionalised within the Health Authority. This may have profound effects for the future development of services and for the perceived relevance of the project for potential clients. Not only may the project be seen as 'detached' from the community, it may be perceived as actively at odds with the community, particularly should it be encouraged to pursue service developments thought applicable by service providers but irrelevant by clients. Much depends on the capacity of the new management structure to develop services according to clients' needs, but for such a process to be adequately facilitated it becomes necessary first, to establish systematic networks for assessing and reviewing clients' needs, and second, to involve outreach and community workers themselves as participants in the management decision making process.

If it is accepted that there is little value in merely providing a 'community front' for existing services, then it is open to question whether the CLASH intervention fulfilled its broad collaborative aims. For commitment to developing innovative ways of contacting clients requires a concomitant commitment to reviewing the accessibility and relevance of existing services on offer. As we have said, there is little point in outreach simply attempting to improve client uptake for the same services which clients have so effectively avoided in the past. The extent to which hard-to-reach clients actually require or perceive a need for existing health services has often been assumed rather than negotiated (perhaps by outreach workers as well as managers). There may be an assumption in many models of outreach that needs among the hard-to-reach for health services far outweigh our own or any other social group. Why should this be so? As we have seen, the extent to which many of CLASH's clients required existing health services was variable, and the proportion of clients referred and positive referral outcomes made were extremely low. This then, may be less an indication of the efficacy of the CLASH project and its ability to make referrals, than it is an indication of the fact that hard-to-reach clients sometimes are unable to perceive a need for, or in fact do not need, services, or are simply not prepared to access services based in the statutory sector. Indeed, it may be considered part of the role of outreach to actively negotiate with clients as to what *are* their service needs and requirements.

If part of the role of outreach work is to identify clients' needs and inform service responses (which is how most managers 'justified' the continued pursuit of referral objectives), then outreach interventions must also be given the encouragement, autonomy and independence to develop their services through the negotiation and participation with clients according to their needs. If, indeed, this results in "changing the nature of what we mean by services", then outreach may have the potential to offer client responsive and community based 'care' oriented services as well as health education and preventive services. This, of course, is precisely what the CLASH project was prevented from doing. This may point not only to the difficulties experienced in managing a project so 'unusual', but also to a reluctance to fund service development perceived as essentially *non-statutory* in orientation. It also points to the need for ongoing and systematic monitoring and evaluation of service delivery in which monitoring of clients' views and perceptions are essential if recommendations for alternative service developments are to be planned and funded. Nonetheless, the evaluation of CLASH showed that there was a need for such services, and that the CLASH team probably knew more than anyone else about how to develop their service responses appropriately. The point here then, is that outreach teams must be committed to providing regular feedback to funders regarding clients' needs for services, and that Health Authority's, should they wish to become involved in such work, must commit themselves to developing services which may not have been traditionally perceived as statutory services. Of course, this may be precisely why hard-to-reach populations are hard-to-reach in the first place. This issue is critical to the future development of outreach services, especially in the context of intersectoral collaboration. If it is impractical for the statutory health sector to manage and develop outreach services effectively, then the question of whether collaborations of this type should be based within the statutory sector at all remains unresolved. Indeed, it may be more appropriate for future similar interventions to be established as independent bodies, perhaps as grant aided companies, with the ability to plan and design their own structures of collaboration between voluntary and statutory sectors, while having commitment (perhaps also financial) from *both* to integrate provision between community based and existing primary care services.

There remains a need for such collaboration as long as there is demand for primary care and medical services - whether they are provided directly in the community or at the hospital. On the basis of our findings, we suggest that CLASH's management structure, although desperately in need of revision, might have allowed the collaboration between voluntary and statutory sectors further chance to function explicitly. Whatever the problems experienced in the management of the CLASH project, the need to 'bridge' gaps, to preserve links with the community, and to involve both voluntary participants and outreach workers as active participants in the management process clearly remain. Without the ability for outreach programmes to remain experimental in design and approach, responsive to clients' health and service needs and sufficiently flexible to adapt and change, then the potential for conflict between the aims and practices of outreach and community intervention, and between real innovation and constraint remains.

ABBREVIATIONS

ACT-UP	AIDS Coalition to Unleash Power
ADAPT	Association for Drug Abuse Prevention and Treatment
AIDS	Acquired Immune Deficiency Syndrome
AWARE	Association for Women's AIDS Research and Education
BHA	Bloomsbury Health Authority
DoH	Department of Health
Cal-PEP	Californian Prostitutes Education Project
CLASH	Central London Action on Street Health
COYOTE	Call Off Your Old Tired Ethics
CUGM	Community Unit General Manager
DASG	District AIDS Steering Group
DDU	Drug Dependency Unit
DHA	District Health Authority
DMO	District Medical Officer
GUM	Genito-Urinary Medicine
HEA	Health Education Authority
HIV	Human Immuno-Deficiency Virus
HIT	Health Improvement Team
JPH	James Pringle House
KAB	Knowledge-Attitudes-Behaviour
NHS	National Health Service
RHA	Regional Health Authority
RWT	Random Weekly Timetable
STD	Sexually Transmitted Disease
THT	Terrence Higgins Trust
UCH	University College Hospital
UCMSM	University College and Middlesex School of Medicine
UGM	Unit General Manager
UK	United Kingdom
US	United States
WECVS	West End Co-ordinated Voluntary Services for Single People

NOTES

CHAPTER ONE
1. The CLASH team can be contacted direct at: CLASH, c/o Margaret Pyke Women's Health Centre, 15 Bateman Buildings, Soho Hospital, Soho Square, London, W1V.

CHAPTER TWO
1. Copies of monitoring instruments are available from the authors.
2. SPSSx is the Statistical Package For Social Scientists.
3. In 1990 Bloomsbury Health Authority merged with Islington Health Authority to form Bloomsbury and Islington Health Authority.

CHAPTER THREE
1. Since the evaluation has been completed discussions have taken place to consider the feasibility of establishing the health and drop-in centre for women prostitutes as outlined in the CLASH team's initial proposal. A weekly satellite STD clinic at the CLASH premises was also established in November 1990.
2. The development and structure of BHA's AIDS services have been described in depth elsewhere (Ferlie and Pettigrew, 1988).
3. These figures are the cumulative number of cases reported to have had contact with the District's services, and do not represent the number of people with AIDS resident in Bloomsbury. As of March 1991, a cumulative total of 130 people living with AIDS were reported to have been resident within the District (CDSC, 1991).
4. The West End Co-ordinated Voluntary Services for Single People was an umbrella organisation which co-ordinated services for yhoung single people in London.
5. The Soho Project was a voluntary based detached outreach and counselling service for young homeless people in central London between 1967 and 1990.
6. The Basement Youth Project is a voluntary based project which has been undertaking youth and community work in West London since the mid 1980s.
7. The Hungerford Drug Project is a voluntary project based in central London, established in 1970 to provide a street based and counselling service for drug users.

8.   The Blenheim Project was founded in 1964 to work with people in crisis in west London. More recently they have specialised in self help drugs advice.

9.   The Piccadilly Advice Centre is a voluntary project providing advice and information on homeless and housing.

10. The Monument Trust, one of the Sainsbury Family Charitable Trusts, provided BHA with funding specifically to develop HIV related community and care services, from which part-funding for CLASH was drawn.

11. CLASH took up premises at the Soho Hospital on June 1st, 1987.

12. Rathbone Place Probation Office.

13. Islington Health Authority's Health Promotion Unit and Angel Project (see note below) have had a regular commitment to undertaking HIV and drugs related training work in Pentonville since 1989.

CHAPTER FIVE

1.   See also Holland, J. (1991) for a discussion of some of the problems with this approach to internal team management.

CHAPTER SIX

1.   Middlesex Lodge, Rufford Street Hostel, Bina Gardens, Haberdashers Hostel. City Roads is a multidisciplinary crisis intervention centre for problem drug users in central London which opened in 1978.

2.   Once data collection on the evaluation was completed, the evaluator was invited by CLASH to take on an advisory role to review and develop systems of internal monitoring.

3.   Streetwise Youth are a voluntary based project in central London providing a detached outreach and drop-in service for young men involved in prostitution

4.   'Cottaging' refers to the male practice of using public toilets as a place (a) to meet other men with a view to having sexual encounters with them, and (b) for having sexual encounters with other men.

5.   'Clipping' refers to the practice in sex work or illicit drugs transactions where a would-be punter, once having paid, is denied the relevant commodity (sex services/drugs).

6.   The Centre Point Night Shelter is a short stay shelter for very young people.

7.   The Health Improvement Team (HIT), based at the National Temperance Hospital aims to prevent the spread of HIV amongst the London-wide drug using population by offering primary health care and health education.

8.   The Margaret Pyke Health Centre offers a family planning service to a largely white middle-class client group of women working in the Central London area. CLASH is located in the same building.

9.   The Angel Project is a voluntary sector drug agency in Islington, providing a range of services for drug users and their families and friends on a drop-in basis.

10.   Rufford Street Hostel is a long stay hostel for over 16 year olds; Greek Street Hostel is a hostel for women.

CHAPTER SEVEN

1.   Concern was expressed by statutory managers that an inordinate number of condoms were distributed to clients. CLASH were allocated a budget of £10,000 per year for condoms alone, although their real yearly expenditure was recently estimated at nearly twice this.

DOCUMENTARY SOURCES

CLASH Team Meeting Minutes, 1986-1990.

CLASH Team Reports to Management, 1986-1990

CLASH Steering Group Minutes, 1987-1990.

CLASH Management Group Minutes, 1987-1990.

CLASH Objectives and Priorities, September 1987.

CLASH Team Terms of Reference, December 1987.

CLASH Aims and Objectives, April 1988.

CLASH Discussion Document: Future initiatives/development over the period covering September 1989-March 1990, August 1989.

CLASH Proposal for a Mobile Unit, undated (mid 1989).

CLASH Proposal for a Women's Drop-in Centre/Clinic in Kings Cross, December 1989.

CLASH Worker's Day and Night Book, 1990-1991.

References in the text to CLASH without further specification refer to CLASH Team minutes and reports.

BIBLIOGRAPHY

Aggleton, P. (1989) 'Evaluating health education about AIDS'. In Aggleton, P., Hart, G., and Davies, P. (eds) *AIDS: Social Representations, Social Practices*, London, Falmer Press.

AIDSCOM (1989) *Education and Evaluation: Partners in AIDS Prevention*, Washington.

Allsop, J. (1984) *Health Policy and the National Health Service*, Harlow, Longman.

Armstrong, D. (1983) *The Political Anatomy of the Body*, Cambridge, Cambridge University Press.

Beattie, A. (1986) 'Community development for health: from practice to theory', *Radical Health Promotion*, 4, 12-18.

Beattie, A. (1991) 'Knowledge and control in health promotion: a test case for social policy and social theory'. In Cabe, J., Calnan, M., and Bury, M. (eds) *The Sociology of the Health Service*, London, Routledge.

Biersteker, S. (1990) 'Promoting safer sex in prostitution: impediments and opportunities'. In Paalman, M. (ed.) *Promoting Safer Sex*, Amsterdam, Swets and Zeitlinger.

Bloor, M., McKeganey, N., and Barnard, M. (1990) 'An ethnographic study of HIV related risk practices among Glasgow rent boys and their clients: report of a pilot study', *AIDS Care*, 2(1), 17-24.

Brown, R., and Margo, G. (1978) 'Health education: can the reformers be reformed?', *International Journal of Health Services*, 8(1), 3-26.

Buning, E., Van Brussel, G., Van Santen, G. (1990) 'The "methadone by bus" project in Amsterdam', *British Journal of Addiction*, 85, 1247-1250.

Buning, E., Van Brussel, G., and Van Santen, G. (1988) 'Amsterdam's drug policy and its implications for controlling needle sharing'. In Battjes, R., and Pickens, R. (eds) *Needle Sharing Among Intravenous Drug Abusers*, Washington, NIDA Research Monograph 80.

Carballo, M., and Rezza, G. (1990) 'AIDS, drugs misuse and the global crisis'. In Strang, J., and Stimson, G. (1990) *AIDS and Drug Misuse*, London, Routledge.

Christmas, J., Lazarus, M., and Lee, M. (1988) 'Health outreach work in the West End of London', *Health Education Journal*, 47(4), 162-163.

Coleman, R., and Curtis, D. (1988) 'Distribution of risk behaviour for HIV infection amongst intravenous drug users', *British Journal of Addiction*, 83, 1331-1334.

Cohen, J., Poole, L. *et al.* (1988) 'Sexual behaviour and HIV infection among 354 sex industry women in a participant-based research and prevention program', paper given at Fourth International Conference on AIDS, Stockholm.

Comella, B., Feltch, F., Kunches, L., *et al* (1989) 'Experience with an anonymous drop-in HIV testing program for intravenous drug users and their contacts'. Paper given at Fifth International Conference on AIDS, Montreal.

Communicable Disease Surveillance Centre Reports, 1991.

Crawford, R. (1977) 'You are dangerous to your health: the ideology and politics of victim blaming', *International Journal of Health Services*, 7(4), 663-679.

Crawford, R. (1980) 'Healthism and the medicalisation of everyday life', *International Journal of Health Services*, 10(3), 365-387.

Dawson, S. (1986) *Analysing organisations*, London: Macmillan Education.

Day, S., Ward, H., and Harris, J. (1988) 'Prostitute women and public health', *British Medical Journal*, 297, 1585.

Day, S., and Ward, H. (1990) 'The Praed Street Project: a cohort of prostitute women in London'. In Plant, M. *(ed.) AIDS, Drugs and Prostitution*, London, Routledge.

Denzin, N. (1970) *The Research Act in Sociology: A Theoretical Introduction to Sociological Method*, London, The Butterworth Group.

Denzin, N. (1978) 'The logic of naturalistic inquiry', in Denzin, N. (ed.) *Sociological method: A sourcebook*, New York, McGraw-Hill.

Delacoste, F., and Alexander, P. (eds) (1987) *Sex Work: Writings by Women in the Sex Industry*, London, Virago.

Des Jarlais, D., and Friedman, S. (1987) 'HIV infection and intravenous drug users: epidemiology and risk reduction'. *AIDS*, 1, 67-76.

Des Jarlais, D. (1989) 'AIDS prevention programs for intravenous drug users: diversity and evolution', *International Review of Psychiatry*, 1(1), 101-108.

Dorn, N. *Management Consultant Report*, 1990.

Doyle, L. (1979) *The Political Economy of Health*, London, Pluto.

Draper, P., Griffiths, J., Dennis, J., and Popay, J. (1980) 'Three types of health education', *British Medical Journal*, 281, 493-495.

Drug Indicators Project (1989) *A Study of Help Seeking and Service Utilisation by Problem Drug Takers*, Research Monograph, London, Institute for the Study of Drug Dependence.

Feeney, F., Brewster, T., Davidson, A., *et al* (1989) 'Access to IV drug users through combined efforts of a public health department and indigenous outreach workers'. Paper given at Fifth International Conference on AIDS, Montreal.

Feldman, H., and Biernacki, P. (1988) 'The ethnography of needle sharing among intravenous drug users and implications for public policies and intervention strategies. In Battjes, R., and Pickens, R. (eds) *Needle Sharing Among Intravenous Drug Abusers*, Washington, NIDA Research Monograph 80.

Ferlie, E., and Pettigrew, A. (1988) *The Management of Change in Bloomsbury DHA: AIDS and Acute Sector Strategy*, University of Warwick, Centre for Corporate Strategy and Change.

Fielding, N., and Fielding, J. (1986) *Linking Data*, London, Sage.

Foucault, M. (1973) *The Birth of the Clinic*, London, Tavistock.

French, J., and Adams, L. (1986) 'Health education: from analysis to synthesis', *Health Education Journal*, 45(2), 71-74.

Friedman, S., Des Jarlais, D., *et al* (1986) 'AIDS health education for intravenous drug users, *Health Education Quarterly*, 13, 383-394.

Friedman, S., De Jong, W., Des Jarlais, D, *et al* (1988) 'Problems and dynamics of organising intravenous drug users for AIDS prevention', *Health Education Research*, 3(1), 49-57.

Friedman, S., Sterk, C., Sufian, M., *et al* (1990) 'Reaching out to injecting drug users'. In Strang, J., and Stimson, G. (eds) *AIDS and Drug Misuse*, London, Routledge.

Gatherer, A., Parfitt, J., Porter, E., *et al.* (1979) *Is Health Education Effective?*, London, Health Education Council.

Gillman, C. (1989) 'Genesis of New York City's experimental needle exchange program', *International Journal of Drugs Policy*, 1(2), 28-32.

George, R., and Hart, G. (1990) 'The Bloomsbury response to HIV and AIDS'. In Pye, M., Kapila, M., *et al* (eds) *Responding to the AIDS Challenge*, London, HEA/Longman.

Guba, E. (1978) *Toward a methodology of naturalistic inquiry in educational evaluation*, (CSE Monograph Series in Evaluation No. 8) Los Angeles, Center for the Study of Evaluation.

Guba, E. and Lincoln, Y. (1981) *Effective evaluation: Improving the usefulness of evaluation results through responsive and naturalistic approaches*, San Francisco, Jossey-Bass.

Hart, G. (1989) 'Needle exchange in central London: operating philosophy and communication strategies', *AIDS Care*, 1(2), 125-134.

Hardy, J. (1981) *Values in Social Policy: Nine Contradictions*, London, Routledge and Kegan Paul.

Hartnoll, R., and Power, R. (1989) 'Why most of Britain's drug users are not looking for help', *Druglink*, 4(2), 8-9.

Hartnoll, R., Rhodes, T., Jones, S., *et al* (1990) *A Survey of HIV Outreach Intervention in the United Kingdom*, University of London, Birkbeck College.

Hassard, A., and Parker, K. (1989) *Preliminary Report on Plymouth Syringe Exchange*, Plymouth Health Authority.

Haw, S. (1985) *Drug Problems in Greater Glasgow*, London, Standing Conference on Drug Abuse.

Holland, J., Ramazanoglu, C., and Scott, S. (1990) *Sex, Risk, and Danger: AIDS Education Policy and Young Women's Sexuality*, Wrap Working Paper 1, London, the Tufnell Press.

Holland, J. (1992) *User Friendly by Design: An Evaluation of a Community Drug Service*, Final Report to the King Edward Hospital Fund, University of London, Birkbeck College, (forthcoming).

Homans, H., and Aggleton, P. (1988) 'Health education about HIV infection and AIDS'. In Aggleton, P., and Homans, H. (eds) *Social Aspects of AIDS*, London, Falmer Press.

Hughes, P., and Crawford, G. (1972) 'A contagious model for researching and intervening in heroin epidemics', *Archives of General Psychiatry*, 27, 585-591.

Jackson, R., Rotkiewicz, L., *et al* (1987) 'A coupon program: drug treatment and AIDS education, unpublished paper, New Jersey State Department of Health.

Jewson, N. (1975) 'Medical knowledge and the patronage system in nineteenth century England', *Sociology*, 83, 309-385.

Johnson, A. (1988) 'Social and behavioural aspects of the HIV epidemic: a review', *Journal of the Royal Statistical Society*, A, 151(1), 99-114.

Kinnell, H. (1989a) *Prostitutes, Their Clients and Risks of HIV infection in Birmingham*, Occasional Paper, Central Birmingham Health Authority.

Kinnell ,H. (1989b) 'Prostitutes, clients and HIV in Birmingham', *AIDS Dialogue*, 4, 8-10.

Klee, H., Faugier, J., Hayes, C., *et al* (1990) 'Sexual partners of injecting drug users: The risk of HIV infection', *British Journal of Addiction*, 85, 4, 413-418.

Klein, R., and Carter, N. (1988) 'Performance measurement: a review of concepts and issues'. In Beeton, D. (ed.) *Performance Measurement: Getting the Concepts Right*, PFF Discussion Paper No. 18.

Maryland Centre Quarterly Surveillance Reports (1989-1990), Mersey Regional Health Authority.

McAuliffe, W., Doering, S., Breer, H., *et al* (1987) 'An evaluation of using ex-addict outreach workers to educate intravenous drug users about AIDS prevention'. Paper given at Fourth International Conference on AIDS, Stockholm.

McDermott, P. (1988) *A Survey of Drug Injectors in the Mersey District*, AIDS Prevention Unit, Mersey Regional Health Authority.

McKeganey, N., Barnard, M., and Watson, H. (1989) 'HIV-related risk behaviour among a non-clinic sample of injecting drug users', *British Journal of Addiction*, 84, 1481-1490.

McKeganey, N., Barnard, M., and Bloor, M. (1990) 'A comparison of HIV-related risk behaviour between female street working prostitutes and male rent boys in Glasgow', *Sociology of Health and Illness*, 12 (3), 274-292.

McKeown, T. (1979) *The Role of Medicine*, Oxford, Oxford University Press.

Morgan Thomas, R., Plant, M. A., Plant, M., *et al* (1989) 'Risks to HIV among workers in the "sex industry": some initial results from a Scottish study', *British Medical Journal*, 299, 148-149.

Moser, A., and Lee, M. (1989) 'Providing health services for women working as prostitutes', CLASH, Bloomsbury Health Authority (unpublished paper).

Narimani, P. (1991) 'International networking in the field of drugs'. Paper given at the Second International Conference on the Reduction of Drug Related Harm, Barcelona.

National Community Health Resource (1989) 'Time for health' conference, Newcastle Upon Tyne.

Newcombe, R. (1989) 'Preventing the spread of HIV infection among and from injecting drug users in the United Kingdom', *International Journal of Drugs Policy,* 1(2), 20-27.

Newcombe, R. (1990) personal communication.

Padian, N. (1988) 'Prostitute women and AIDS: epidemiology', *AIDS,* 2, 413-419.

Patton, C. (1988) 'Inventing African AIDS', *City Limits,* 363, 85.

Patton, M. (1987) *How to use qualitative methods in evaluation,* London, Sage.

Patton, M. (1990) *Qualitative Evaluation Methods,* Second Edition, London, Sage.

Pearson, G. (1973) 'Social work as the privatised solution of public ills', *British Journal of Social Work,* 3(2), 209-227.

Porter, R. (1986) 'History says no to the policeman's response to AIDS', *British Medical Journal,* 2, 1589-1590.

Porter, D., and Porter, R. (1988) 'The enforcement of health: the British debate'. In Fee, E., and Fox, D. (eds) *AIDS: The Burdens of History,* Los Angeles, University of California Press.

Power, R., Hartnoll, R. L., and Daviaud, E. (1988) 'Drug injecting, AIDS and risk behaviour: potential for change and intervention strategies', *British Journal of Addiction,* 83, 649-654.

Power, R. (1989) 'Drugs and the media: prevention campaigns and television'. In MacGregor, S. *(ed.) Drugs and British Society,* London, Routledge.

Reid, T. (1989) Editorial, *International Working Group on AIDS and IV Drug Use Newsletter,* 4(3), 9.

Research Bureau Limited (1989) *Anti Misuse of Drugs Campaign Evaluation. Report of Findings of Stages I-VII,* London, RBL.

Rhodes, T., and Shaughnessy, R. (1990) 'Compulsory screening: advertising AIDS in Britain, 1986-89', *Policy and Politics,* 18(1), 55-61.

Rhodes, T., Holland, J., Hartnoll, R., *et al.* (1990) 'Reaching the hard to reach', *Druglink,* 5(6), 12-15.

Rhodes, T., and Hartnoll, R. (1991) 'Reaching the hard to reach: models of HIV outreach health education'. In Aggleton, P., Davies, P., and Hart, G. (eds) *AIDS: Responses, Intervention and Care,* London, Falmer Press.

Rhodes, T., Hartnoll, R., and Johnson, A. (with Holland, J. and Jones, S.) (1991a) *Out of the Agency and on to the Streets,* London, Institute for the Study of Drug Dependence Research Monograph 2.

Rhodes, T., Holland, J., Hartnoll, R., *et al* (1991b) 'HIV outreach in Britain', *Druglink,* 6(3), 12-14.

Rhodes, T., Holland, J., Hartnoll, R., and Johnson, A. (1991c) *HIV Outreach Health Education: National and International Perspectives*, University of London, Birkbeck College.

Roberts, T. (1989) 'A street counselling service for women prostitutes'. Paper given at RSM Forum on Medical Communication 'Communication Issues in HIV and AIDS, London.

Robinson, T. (1989) *London's Homosexual Male Prostitutes: Power, Peer Groups and HIV*, Project Sigma Working Paper No. 12, South Bank Polytechnic.

Safe Project (1990) *Quarterly Reports*, Central Birmingham Health Authority.

Sheffield AIDS Education Project (1990) 'Review of detached work with women prostitutes', Sheffield AIDS Education Project (unpublished paper).

Silverman, D. (1990) 'The social organisation of HIV counselling'. In Aggleton, P., Davies, P., and Hart, G. (eds) *AIDS: Individual, Cultural and Policy Dimensions*, London, Falmer Press.

Smithies, J., and Webster, G. (1991) 'Evaluating community development and health work'. Paper given at the British Sociological Association Annual Conference 'Health and Society', Manchester.

Sorge, R. (1991) 'Act-up before you shoot up: "underground" needle exchange in New York'. Paper given at Second International Conference on the Reduction of Drug Related Harm, Barcelona.

Stimson, G., Alldritt, L., Dolan, K., *et al* (1988) *Injecting Equipment Exchange Schemes: Final Report*, University of London, Goldsmiths' College.

Tomlinson, D. (1991) 'Screening for sexually transmitted disease in London-based male prostitutes', *Genito-Urinary Medicine*, 67, 103-106.

Tones, K. (1981) 'Health education: prevention or subversion?', *Royal Society of Health Journal*, 3, 114-117.

Tones, K., Tilford, S., and Robinson, Y. (1990) *Health Education: Effectiveness and Efficiency*, London, Chapman and Hall.

Treichler, P. (1987) 'AIDS, homophobia and biomedical discourse: an epidemic of signification', *Cultural Studies*, 1(3), 263-305.

Tuckett, D. (1973) 'Choices for health education: a sociological view'. In Sutherland, I. *(ed.) Health Education: Perspectives and Choices*, London, Allen and Unwin.

Van den Hoek, J., Coutinhor, R., *et al* (1988) 'Prevalence and risk factors of HIV infection amongst drug users and prostitutes in Amsterdam', *AIDS*, 2, 55-60.

Veenker, J. (1990) 'Safer sex among gay men: a continuous effort'. In Paalman, M. (ed.) *Promoting Safer Sex*, Amsterdam, Swets and Zeitlinger.

Verbeek, H., and Van der Zijden, T. (1987) 'The Red Thread: whore's movement in Holland'. In Delacoste, F., and Alexander, P. (eds) *Sex Work: Writings by Women in the Sex Industry*, London, Virago.

Watney, S. (1988a) 'Missionary politics: AIDS, Africa and race', *Differences: A Feminist Journal of Cultural Studies*, 1(1).

Watney, S. (1988b) 'The spectacle of AIDS'. In Crimp, D. *(ed.) AIDS: Cultural Analysis, Cultural Activism*, London, MIT Press.

Watney, S. (1988c) 'Visual AIDS: advertising ignorance'. In Aggleton, P., and Homans, H. (eds) *Social Aspects of AIDS*, London, Falmer Press.

Webster, G. (1991) 'Community development and health: a collective approach to social change'. Paper given at the British Sociological Association Annual Conference 'Health and Society', Manchester.

Wiebel, W. (1988) 'Combining ethnographic and epidemiologic methods in targeted AIDS interventions: the Chicago model. In Battjes, R., and Pickens, R. (eds) *Needle Sharing Among Intravenous Drug Abusers*, Washington, NIDA Research Monograph 80.

Wiebel, W. (1991) 'Indigenous outreach to intravenous drug users'. Paper given at Second International Conference on the Reduction of Drug Related Harm, Barcelona.

APPENDIX A

SUMMARY OF FINDINGS, CONCLUSIONS AND RECOMMENDATIONS

Central London Action on Street Health (CLASH) is a model of HIV outreach health education managed through collaboration between voluntary and statutory health sectors with the broad aim of providing an integrated service provision between the two sectors.

Management structure and functioning: Core findings

Aims and objectives

* The original aims of the CLASH project were to:
    (a) conduct detached outreach work with hard-to-reach populations in order to provide health education information and advice, particularly in relation to HIV infection and AIDS;
    (b) develop "accessible, relevant and appropriate" health education materials;
    (c) facilitate referral and access into health services for target groups without easy access to statutory and voluntary health services.

* At the time of writing, these broad aims have been further specified and clarified and involve:
    (a) contacting those not accessing health services, particularly men and women working in the sex industries, drug users and injectors, young homeless people and prisoners;
    (b) training staff working with the above target groups;
    (c) providing and facilitating referrals to health services, voluntary organisations and social services, and identifying requirements for improved access to service provision;
    (d) providing health education, advice and counselling, particularly about HIV infection and AIDS;
    (e) providing prevention materials: syringes, needles, condoms, spermicide, lubricants;
    (f) developing appropriate health education literature and materials.

Management structure
*   The project's management structure was designed to facilitate
        collaboration between statutory and voluntary sectors. It consisted of
        four components:
            (a) the Steering Group which consisted of equal numbers of
                representatives from each of the sectors and which aimed to
                manage the project's overall strategy and policy;
            (b) the Management Group which consisted of statutory
                representatives including Bloomsbury Health Authority's
                (BHA's) Unit General Manager (UGM) which was responsible
                for the project's day-to-day management and administration;
            (c) the Voluntary Sub-Group which consisted of voluntary
                representatives and which met for a short period to provide
                support and direction on outreach working practice;
            (d) the CLASH team which consisted of four full-time workers and
                who organised themselves as a collective with equal and
                shared responsibility for the work and internal functioning of
                the team.

Management functioning: problems of design
*   The management structure's functioning proved problematic at
        three distinctive levels of the management process: the internal
        functioning of the team's collective; the interface between the team
        and management; the interface between voluntary and statutory
        managers.
*   A variety of factors influenced these problems within and between
        the three levels of the management process. They are summarised
        as follows:
            (a) lack of management definition and direction for internal team
                organisation and management processes;
            (b) lack of management interface and accountability between the
                CLASH team and Steering Group;
            (c) lack of management interface, responsibility and accountability
                between the CLASH team and Management Group;
            (d) lack of clear lines of responsibility in power of organisation
                between voluntary and statutory sector participants on the
                Steering Group;
            (e) lack of clear lines of responsibility and accountability between
                the Steering Group and Management Group.

Management functioning: problems of circumstance
* Feeding from the problems in management structure were problems of circumstance created by the act of collaborating in the management of the project:
    (a) competing ideologies of management between the principles of collective working and NHS hierarchy;
    (b) competing ideologies between styles of work and management between workers and statutory managers;
    (c) competing ideologies between styles of work and management between voluntary and statutory sector managers;
    (d) collusion in ideologies between styles of work and management between workers and voluntary managers.

New management structures
* Following the management consultant's recommendations endorsed by the Steering Group the CLASH team will be re-structured hierarchically within the Authority. This will involve:
    (a) appointing a co-ordinator within the CLASH team who is accountable to a series of NHS line managers;
    (b) dissolving the Management Group;
    (c) replacing the Steering Group with an Advisory Group of statutory and voluntary managers with no decision making power.

Management structure and functioning: Recommendations

The evaluation identified a number of possible suggestions for improvement in relation to the problems encountered in management structure functioning:
* Appointment of a team leader with the responsibility of organising, implementing and directing internal team management procedures. The team leader could organise internal management procedures according to his/her and the team's wishes, either hierarchically or in a task-oriented non-hierarchical fashion. Should the team be organised in a non-hierarchical task-oriented fashion, workers should be encouraged to realise their own areas of interest and expertise while providing direct feed back to the team, thus allowing for an element of reflexivity in team functioning. The team leader, responsible for its smooth running and effectiveness would be accountable to BHA line managers in the NHS hierarchy.

*   Appointment of worker with some NHS experience within the
      CLASH team to assist in enabling the team the skills to communicate
      and negotiate both directly and effectively with statutory managers.
*   The appointment of the team leader replaces the need for the
      Management Group to manage on everyday and administrative
      matters. There is no longer a need for the Management Group. The
      team leader, responsible and accountable to NHS line managers
      becomes responsible for the everyday and administrative functioning
      of the CLASH project.
*   The Steering Group should preserve its aim of collaboration
      between voluntary and statutory participants with the aim of integrating
      service provision between the two sectors. The newly proposed
      Advisory Group takes away the decision making power of voluntary
      participants. We recommend that it is important for voluntary
      participants involved and experienced in community based work to
      retain equal decision making power in a project of this type to ensure
      that the direction of outreach services are relevant and feasible to
      client and community needs and to ensure that the project continues
      to provide an integrated voluntary-statutory network of service
      provision. This will involve re-negotiating the lines of power and
      responsibility between the voluntary and statutory participants
      involved. This is essential to ensure that the power, interest and
      commitment of both sectors is retained throughout. Clear lines of
      accountability should also be drawn between the CLASH team,
      CLASH team leader and voluntary participants on the Steering
      Group, and voluntary representatives (as managers) should be
      made directly accountable to fellow members of the Steering Group
      and not to members of the CLASH team.
*   The newly proposed Advisory Group recommends that the team
      co-ordinator takes on the negotiation role on behalf of CLASH with
      one (rotating) CLASH worker present at these meetings. We
      recommend that it is essential for outreach workers themselves to
      have an active and fully participative role in this management
      process as they are most aware of clients' needs and the feasibility
      of service options. Without the full participation of voluntary managers
      and outreach workers in the decision making process, much of the
      responsibility for ensuring that the management process 'works' to
      the clients' advantage depends on the individual abilities of the co-
      ordinator to instrument change within the Health Authority. This is
      neither likely or satisfactory. Without building into the structure
      mechanisms to ensure that the service is developed according to

clients' needs, there may be a tendency for the project to be managed in a top-down and prescriptive fashion.

* Problems arising through circumstance rather than through management design but which contributed to the problematic functioning of the management structure may have been alleviated in part had the collaboration had the flexibility to move between management styles, to learn and adapt accordingly; and the rigidity to prevent conflicts and tensions disrupting the basic decision making function of the management process.

* Our recommended management structure, which is an intermediate version of the existing and newly proposed structure, would be committed to encouraging real innovation in practice, permitting:

(a) the possibility for non-hierarchical task oriented management within the team if so desired (overseen by team leader);

(b) accountability within the team concerning internal team management;

(c) a direct interface and accountability between the team and Steering Group;

(d) immediate accountability and direction between the team and Health Authority through the team leader on issues of day to day management and administration;

(e) the direction of project work to be organised through collaboration, with a commitment to pursuing service development as required, so preserving the aims of the project to 'bridge gaps' by integrating responses to service provision.

Outreach contact and service delivery: core findings

Total outreach contacts

* A total of 741 clients were contacted through detached outreach work throughout the monitoring period, 1st January 1988 to 31st July 1990. A total of 1383 separate outreach contacts were made with these clients: 533 clients were contacted once and 188 were re-contacted an average of three times each.

* The above total contacts do not include the team's contact with clients through training and peripatetic work. It must also be recognised that it is likely that the figures are a slight under-estimate.

New clients' characteristics

*   Of the 741 new clients contacted, 46% were female and 54% male, with one person of cross-gender. The average age of clients was 23 years, with the vast majority (83%) described as 'White British'.

*   Nearly all (97%) new contacts were made 'face to face', and 86% were 'cold' contacts. Of the face to face contacts, 85% were made via detached outreach work - on the streets (41%), in pubs (23%), at working women's flats (13%), in cafes (4%) or at other locations (4%).

*   Two thirds (67%) of female clients were known to be working as women prostitutes, 40% of male clients as rent boys, 28% of clients were known to be using illicit drugs, 22% were known to be injecting, and 20% were known to be 'homeless' or in insecure accommodation. Only thirteen new clients were known not to be in any of these categories. It is difficult to make any realistic assessment of the extent to which those 'not known' to be working as prostitutes or to be using drugs, were actually involved in prostitution or drug use.

*   One fifth (20%) of clients were known to be in current contact with other agencies, 21% were known not to be, and for 59% of clients this information was unknown. Where this information was unknown, clients were more likely not to be in contact, particularly with statutory based services. Female clients were less likely than male clients to be in contact with other services.

*   Two thirds (63%) of women prostitutes were contacted in the King's Cross area, and 30% were made with women working from flats in Soho. Most rent boys (59%) were contacted in Soho, almost all (92%) of which were contacted in a pub commonly frequented by rent boys.

*   Three quarters (77%) of the new clients known to be using illicit drugs were also injecting. Clients injecting were more likely to be male and older. Where known, half (46%) of rent boys and 36% of women prostitutes were using illicit drugs, and 15% of rent boys and 33% of women prostitutes were injecting. This is an unusually high proportion of prostitutes involved in drug use, and this is partly a reflection of the concentrated locations where CLASH contacted clients.

*   There is little reliable data about new clients' vulnerability to HIV infection. However, 52% of clients were thought to be using condoms 'usually' with their sexual partners, 21% 'always' and 28% 'never'. Women prostitutes were slightly more likely to be using condoms

more regularly with their punters than rent boys. Of clients injecting drugs (22%), 4% were known to be sharing, 16% not to be sharing and for 80% this information was unknown.
* For 12% of clients it was known whether or not they had been tested for HIV antibody. Of these, 25% were HIV antibody positive, 19% antibody negative, 9% were tested with results at the time unknown, and 47% remained untested. The findings support those from elsewhere which suggest there is little evidence in the UK linking seropositivity to women prostitutes who do not inject drugs. Conversely, they suggest higher risks associated with the rent scene.

Service provision
* When conducting outreach contacts, condoms were distributed to 92% of women prostitutes, 73% of rent boys and 49% of drug injectors. 75% of drug injectors were provided with clean injecting equipment.
* CLASH made arrangements for further contact with 13% of new clients, and made referral arrangements with 12%, the majority of which were to statutory organisations. The proportion of positive referral outcomes to referrals made is unknown, although is likely to be under 20%.

Re-contacted clients' characteristics

* The vast majority (96%) of the 642 re-contacts made with re-contacted clients (188) were face to face contacts, but were slightly more likely to be client initiated (38% as opposed to 11%) and slightly shorter in duration (11 minutes as opposed to 13 minutes) than on new contact.
* Unlike new contacts, most (72%) of the 188 clients re-contacted were female, while their average age was the same as on new contact (23 years).
* Over half (56%) of the clients re-contacted were known to be working as women prostitutes, 9% to be working as rent boys, and 25% to be injecting drugs. 10% of clients were both working as women prostitutes and injecting, and 2% were working as rent boys and injecting. This means that of new clients, 46% of women prostitutes were re-contacted, 11% of rent boys and 30% of drug injectors.

*   There was an increased likelihood of contacting women prostitutes
     on re-contacts (56% as opposed to 30% of new contact), and a
     corresponding decrease in contacts with rent boys (9% as opposed
     to 22% of new contacts). The extent to which drug injectors were
     contacted was similar (25% as opposed to 22%).
*   There was little evidence of change in clients' HIV and health
     behaviour either between new contacts and re-contacts or across re-
     contacts. This was in part because the information was unavailable
     to outreach workers over time, in part because the extent of knowledge
     about clients differed between workers contacting the same client,
     and in part because the numbers of re-contacts per client were
     relatively low. It was not feasible to attribute the few changes which
     did occur (which were slightly more positive than negative in direction)
     to the CLASH intervention.

Service provision
*   On three quarters (75%) of re-contacts condoms were distributed,
     in almost all cases to women prostitutes. Injecting equipment was
     distributed on 17% of re-contacts, lubricants on 28%, and spermicide
     on 11%.
*   CLASH made arrangements for further contact on 17% of re-
     contacts (110 times) with 40 clients; an average of three arrangements
     per client. Where arrangements were made, 85 subsequent re-
     contacts occurred (a 75% success rate), and 28 clients were never
     re-contacted. Of the remaining occasions were arrangements were
     not made, 347 re-contacts occurred. As the arrangements made with
     clients were usually for a specific reason, as opposed to being re-
     contacted on following outreach sessions, this can be considered
     encouraging.
*   Arrangements for referral elsewhere were made on 10% of re-
     contacts (64 times) with 39 clients. Most of these were with women
     prostitutes, and most were to statutory based services. To CLASH's
     knowledge 37% of these referrals were taken up by clients. This is
     probably an over estimate. It was not possible to make an accurate
     assessment of the proportion of referrals taken up.

Outreach contact and service delivery: conclusions

*   The CLASH team allocated approximately half (48%) of their total
     weekly project time to undertaking work directly with clients, of which

35% was allocated to detached work. Of the remaining half (52%) of their time, 45% was allocated to project management and administration. In practice, as a result of problems in internal team organisation and management, the team actually invested even less time than that allocated to client based work (approximately 27%).

* The team's peripatetic outreach work was well established in both women's prisons and hostels for the homeless. The project was effective in reaching clients out-of-contact with health services in these institutions. The time allocated to such work was sufficient, although the time actually invested was variable.

* Differing perceptions and expectations of the team's extent of contact with clients existed between the critical actors involved. Statutory representatives, while recognising the need for a long period to establish outreach work, were more likely than voluntary representatives to have concerns over the numbers of clients contacted through outreach work.

* The team might have achieved a greater level of outreach contact with clients had they invested greater project time in detached outreach work, increased the use of indigenous outreach workers and liaised with police as to their presence and purpose.

* The team's organisation of outreach work on the basis of working in pairs and the matching of workers' characteristics to those of their clients on aspects of gender and sexuality should be encouraged. However, it should also be noted that this inhibited the sharing of work within the team, where workers became protective of their own individual areas of work interest.

* The target groups of street based sex industry workers and drug injectors in central London are considerably more transient than in other parts of the UK. They are thus harder-to-reach and require the use of imaginative and aggressive contacting strategies. The probabilities of achieving client contacts, and especially re-contacts, will therefore remain far lower than elsewhere in the UK, and so the level of time, resources and workers invested as a function of outreach contact will be far higher.

* The project effectively reached intended target populations, although non-prostitute drug users and drug injectors were under-targeted and subsequently under-contacted. The degree to which populations contacted were vulnerable to HIV infection varied, with women prostitutes working from flats in Soho being considered the least vulnerable to health problems in the opinion of the CLASH team. The targeting by the team of those considered less vulnerable

to infection relative to those considered at greater risk was well balanced and effective.

* Although difficult to determine, the project appeared to reach those with little or no contact with health services. It is encouraging that clients contacted were less likely to be in contact with statutory based services than with voluntary based services.

* The rate of client referral was low, although referrals were more likely to be directed towards statutory based services. Where it was possible to determine, the proportion of positive referral outcomes to referrals made was small. This seemed as much an indicator of the accessibility and relevance of services on offer, as it did about the CLASH project's ability to make effective referrals.

* The problems experienced in achieving referral objectives were related to the perceived and experienced inaccessibility and irrelevance of statutory services, the inability of CLASH to achieve effective referral mechanisms within the Health Authority, the structural constraints which CLASH faced in effecting appropriate change within the Health Authority, and the lack of perceived need and desire among clients to access statutory services.

* Differing perceptions and expectations existed between critical actors as to the balance between objectives of referral and objectives to provide *in situ* street health education and services. Some statutory representatives tended to see the achievement of referral as "justification" for outreach work, while voluntary representatives viewed outreach as a primary objective in its own right. The CLASH team, finding referral difficult to achieve, 'naturally' developed the emphasis of their outreach work towards *in situ* service provision.

* The CLASH team effectively distributed condoms, injecting equipment, lubricants, spermicide and project cards when undertaking detached outreach work. The weekly drop-in service also provided an effective opportunity for the distribution of preventive materials.

* On detached outreach contacts, the extent to which the team was able to provide for clients' HIV health needs was varied. As far as the team's work with rent boys was concerned, the team effectively created opportunities to advise on safer sex and condom use, but were less effective in doing so concerning safer drug use and injecting techniques. No observations were possible on detached outreach with women prostitutes.

* On detached outreach contacts with rent boys, the team was effective in providing health education advice where the opportunities arose, as well as more general advice about where clients could seek

help on problems to do with housing, legal or finance.
* On detached outreach contacts, the extent to which the team were able to provide for clients' more general health needs was limited. This was a function of the style and brevity of outreach contacts, the lack of time and opportunity for clients to recognise their health needs, the fact that most clients had more pressing needs than concerns about STDs or HIV (housing, money, food), that clients' simply had a lack of desire or were unwilling to consider their health problems, and that clients had no desire or were unwilling to consider making appointments to access health services.
* As a function of project time and resources and of the opportunities the outreach contact provides for *in situ* health education and opportunities to cater for clients' HIV specific and general health needs, the outreach contact may not appear to be cost-effective. The commitment to reaching the hard-to-reach, however, may demand such resources, even when positive returns appear less visible in comparison with more conventional modes of health care, and this may be considered part of the essence - or part of "the problem" - of outreach work.

Service development
* Largely as a result of finding referral objectives unworkable, the CLASH team made attempts to develop their services towards a more comprehensive and independent *in situ* model of service delivery rather than attempt to continue to forge links with existing services. These moves were most clearly expounded in their proposals for a mobile outreach unit and a women's drop-in and health centre in King's Cross.
* Differences in perception regarding the direction that CLASH's services should take existed between critical actors. These differences represented wider differences in expectations of outreach work and service provision, and between more 'top-down' and 'bottom-up' styles of service delivery. It is precisely the 'community-professional' conflicts in conceptualisations of health and service provision which the CLASH model attempted to acknowledge in combining such approaches, which hampered the development of its services.

Outreach contact and service delivery: Recommendations

*   The team needs to re-consider the balance between particular project activities in terms of allocating appropriate project time and resources. We recommend that perhaps as much as 65% of the project's time be allocated to detached outreach work, and proportionately less time to other project activities, particularly team management and project administration. We also emphasise that clearer lines of accountability should be drawn between workers to ensure that the time allocated to particular areas of work is actually invested in practice.

*   To improve the team's rate of outreach contact with clients, greater project time needs to be allocated to detached outreach work and more aggressive outreach strategies should be employed (for example, a mobile outreach unit). We also recommend the increased employment of indigenous workers, particularly as part-time and sessional workers, and these might also include current sex industry workers and drug users. The project might also consider liaising with police in the hope of facilitating the ease with which outreach contacts are made.

*   The balance achieved between the targeting of women prostitutes and rent boys who were considered more and less vulnerable to HIV infection and in need of health services should continue. Unless greater time is allocated to detached outreach work, the team should not consider the targeting of women prostitutes and rent boys working as escorts, as masseurs or from home. There is an urgent need, however, for the team to re-evaluate its work with drug users and drug injectors. Detached outreach sessions working specifically with drug injectors (including the targeting of non-prostitute drug injectors) should be undertaken, and to facilitate this, workers (full-time, sessional or indigenous) should be employed with specific skills and expertise in this area. To alleviate some of the team's frustration and concern in this area, we recommend staff training concentrating on practical issues of drug related health behaviour, and this should be provided externally should the appropriate expertise not be found within the team.

*   We recommend that the objectives of referral in future be seen as a secondary outcome of outreach work, while encouraging effective referral mechanisms for those that require it. This requires an element of mutual trust and confidence between the Health Authority and the CLASH team. In this respect, the Health Authority should aim

to facilitate the arrangement of referral procedures, and the provision of flexible and accessible services. The CLASH team should provide regular feed back to the Health Authority about their clients wishes and demands, and the teams' proposals and recommendations for service improvement. There is a need to develop methods of client needs assessment, which allow for the systematic monitoring of clients' own views and perceptions of the accessibility and relevance of statutory services (rather than those presumed to be the case by workers or managers).

* If the Health Authority is committed to reaching and providing for the hard-to-reach, then it is vital that their outreach services should be permitted to develop in response to clients' demands. Thus, to facilitate objectives of referral there must be strong commitment to expecting and accepting change to the style and nature of existing service delivery.

* The team's Friday drop-in service was effective in providing opportunities for the team to lend advice, information and counselling to clients. It also allowed further opportunity for clients to discuss their general health needs and service needs, outside of the constraints of the street outreach contact. This was especially the case given that clients were more likely to take up arrangements to come to the CLASH office than they were to take up referrals made to elsewhere. We therefore recommend that this service should continue, if possible be expanded, and that outreach workers stress its importance when delivering services to clients. Should greater time be invested in detached outreach work, then there is no doubt that greater time should also be invested in client drop-in. The more flexible and available the CLASH team are able to make themselves to clients the more accessible they become.

* One of the main problems facing the CLASH team when attempting to encourage clients to consider or recognise their potential health problems or health service needs, was that clients' most immediate needs were for shelter, accommodation, money, food, legal advice, emotional support and so on. In this context, concerns of clients about STDs or HIV were of secondary importance. In the light of this, we make two recommendations.

First, that it is fundamental that outreach workers are competent in their knowledge and skills around issues of homelessness (where to refer, realistic options for shelter etc.). Staff training should be encouraged, and this should be provided externally should the appropriate expertise not be found within the team.

Second - and most importantly - we recommend that the focus and purpose of the outreach contact be reviewed critically by workers and managers involved. There is little point in the project specifically aiming to cater for clients' HIV and health needs when there exist far more pressing needs and obstacles from the clients' perspective. Clients' needs should therefore be viewed more holistically where HIV and health needs are seen as only one need of many. As it is clearly impractical for one outreach project to cater for all clients' complete social, welfare and medical needs, this requires careful planning and negotiation with neighbouring outreach projects as to precisely who aims to contact whom, and who aims to provide what. With a competent working knowledge of the appropriate issues involved (especially including housing, financial, legal), and with a network of integrated services to turn to, individual projects and outreach workers might feel more confident and able to offer their clients both realistic advice and tangible choices upon which to act.

*   We recommend that the outreach contact should be considered a cost-effective method to reach and provide services for the hard-to-reach. Relative to more conventional styles of service delivery the outreach contact runs the risk of being considered cost-ineffective. If there is commitment for reaching the hard-to-reach and providing the unserviced with services they consider relevant and applicable, then this is inevitably going to cost comparatively more than providing for those already serviced. Considerations as to the cost effectiveness of outreach should therefore be sensitive to the purpose in hand and the criteria of judgement employed. In order to facilitate this process and the planning of appropriate models of service provision, there is a need for direct and ongoing feed back of monitoring and evaluation to funding bodies on the effectiveness of particular outreach strategies and interventions.

Service development
*   We recommend that the fundamental aims of outreach to provide services for hard-to-reach populations should not be over looked. It is axiomatic that outreach interventions should remain flexible in design and responsive in approach. It is important to recognise the limitations of existing service responses in appearing relevant or useful to some client groups. It is also important to realise the potential for outreach to provide *in situ* and community based 'care' oriented services as well as preventive services. In this sense, mobile outreach units and community based health centres are

clearly 'outreach' in their approach as they aim to provide the services required according to clients needs. We recommend that should statutory health sectors remain committed to reaching the hard-to-reach, which we stress is very encouraging, there should be some expectation and commitment to funding styles of service delivery which may be perceived to be essentially non-statutory in orientation. There is a need to define hard-to-reach populations and their needs and demands on their own terms, and not simply in the terms of pre-existing service responses. This should be the starting point for outreach interventions. Only on this basis, can outreach intervention hope to achieve its aims of effectively providing for hard-to-reach clients' health needs.

* In relation to the CLASH project, we recommend that the team's proposals for a mobile outreach unit and women's drop-in and health centre be endorsed. The mobile unit should have the dual purpose of catering for the team's needs for increased mobility and for providing direct and immediate STD and medical check-up and advice by doctors and nurses employed for the purpose (rather like Amsterdam's methadone buses). The women's centre, as CLASH's proposals suggest, should have the dual purpose of providing for women's immediate health care needs as well as providing drop-in for advice and information (rather like the mobile contact centre in Utrecht). The feasibility and effectiveness of these interventions should be carefully piloted, monitored and reviewed.

Evaluation
* As models of HIV outreach intervention remain innovative and experimental, there is a continued need for the systematic and rigorous monitoring and evaluation of outreach work and service delivery to shed light on the future direction and development of outreach services. At its most basic, we recommend this should include process performance indicators to monitor the extent and nature of outreach contact and project activities. Ideally evaluation designs should be tailored to service needs and developments, combine qualitative and quantitative methods, and incorporate both process and outcome measures. Evaluations may be most effective if they are integrated into the overall design of a project from the outset, if they are negotiated and developed in conjunction with workers and managers, if they directly include the clients of the service, and if they employ action-oriented research methods which are able to inform the ongoing formulation and implementation of

interventionist strategy. There is a need to assess critically the feasibility and effectiveness of evaluation methods as they apply to the evaluation of outreach and community based interventions.

Evaluation of CLASH: Final conclusion and recommendation

*   Finally, we conclude that the CLASH model of HIV outreach health education was an innovative and proactive attempt to collaborate between statutory and voluntary health sectors with the explicit aim of providing an integrated service provision for hard-to-reach populations. Aware of the potential for conflict between differing and competing approaches to health and service provision in a collaboration of this type, and on the basis of the findings presented in this evaluation, we recommend that future similar collaborations should be encouraged, but may only be feasible given careful attention to structures of management, the precise roles which participants are to play, and the commitment to developing truly innovative and community-based services.

INDEX OF NAMES

SUBJECT INDEX

NOTES ON THE AUTHORS

Tim Rhodes
is a Research Fellow in the Department of Politics and Sociology,
Birkbeck College, University of London;

Janet Holland
is a Senior Research Officer in the Social Science Research Unit,
University of London Institute of Education;

Richard Hartnoll
is a Scientific Research Fellow in the Department of Epidemiology,
Institut Municipal d'Investigacio Medica, Barcelona.